358.

359. **THE**

360. **DIALECTICAL**

361. **BEHAVIOR**

362. **THERAPY**

363. **WELLNESS**

364. **PLANNER**

365. **365** days of healthy living for your body, mind, and spirit

UNHOOKED BOOKS
An Imprint of High Conflict Institute Press
Scottsdale, Arizona

Publisher's Note
This publication is designed to provide accurate and
authoritative information about the subject matters covered.
It is sold with the understanding that neither the author
nor publisher are rendering legal, mental health, medical,
or other professional services, either directly or indirectly.
If expert assistance, legal services, or counseling is needed,
the services of a competent professional should be sought.
Neither the author nor the publisher shall be liable or
responsible for any loss or damage allegedly arising as a
consequence of your use or application of any information or
suggestions in this book.

Unhooked Books, LLC
7701 E. Indian School Rd., Ste. F
Scottsdale, AZ 85251
www.unhookedbooks.com

ISBN: 978-1-936268-86-3
eISBN: 978-1-936268-87-0

Library of Congress Control Number: 2015939718

Cover and book design by Julian Leon / themissive.com
Printed in the United States

ACKNOWLEDGEMENTS

For my sister, Cheryl A. Honaker, the best
DBT skills coach I could ever ask for.

FOREWORD

By **Blaise Aguirre, MD**

Some years ago, I worked with a young woman who had a hard time tracking her experience from day-to-day. She used the diary cards I gave her, but because of crisis-ridden life, she couldn't keep her diary cards together and it was hard to measure her progress week-over-week. She moved to trying to track her emotions and behaviors on her smartphone, but again, having to scroll back and forth between the most recent week and what happened 16 weeks ago (for instance) was cumbersome. She loved to journal, so I suggested that she do that instead; however, even though this was a more productive way of monitoring, it had two drawbacks. The first was that there were days she would write an entire novel, and days that she would write a single sentence.

I wished that there were a way for her to consistently be able to report on her journey to healing. She needed the benefit of a journal with all its pages in one tome, the utility of a diary card with easy prompts to focus her attention on specific target behaviors, and the practicality of a smartphone, keeping days in order without skipping tasks or days.

Amanda Smith has done just that with *The Dialectical Behavior Therapy Wellness Planner: 365 Days of Healthy Living for Your Body, Mind, and Spirit*. It is a practical tool for the emotionally sensitive person looking for an easier way to track your emotions and behavior as well as monitor progress over time.

The day-to-dayness of the planner brings gentle structure that does not overwhelm with burdensome demands. At the same time, it makes the skills from dialectical behavioral therapy (DBT) accessible for in-the-moment review as well allowing the user to continue to monitor their progress with self-assessment tools.

This is a wonderful little planner. Individuals will find it to be an important and personal yardstick on their journey to recovery. I also imagine giving it to members of a DBT skills group as a graduation present as a practical gift and a memento the utility of which will last a lifetime.

Blaise Aguirre, MD
Medical Director
3East DBT-Continuum
McLean Hospital
Assistant Professor of Psychiatry
Harvard Medical School
http://www.3east.org/

CONTENTS

WHY DIALECTICAL BEHAVIOR THERAPY?

I love dialectical behavior therapy. As a highly sensitive person who experiences my emotions intensely, learning dialectical behavior therapy (or DBT) has made a profound and lasting difference in my own life.

Now that I'm a social worker, I continue to use the skills I learned in DBT every single day but I'm also in the position of sharing my joyful enthusiasm for this compassionate and highly-effective treatment with others.

DBT was originally developed by **Marsha Linehan**—a psychologist at the University of Washington—to help people who were diagnosed with borderline personality disorder. However, the treatment has now been adapted for individuals suffering from depression, anxiety, bipolar disorder, post-traumatic stress disorder, eating disorders, addictions, and even attention deficit hyperactivity disorder.

While DBT is based in cognitive behavior therapy (or CBT), Dr. Linehan found that a key to her clients' success was to balance both acceptance and change in their lives.

It was because of this reason that she added mindfulness, validation strategies, and dialectics to standard CBT. Because the goal of DBT is to help people create lives worth living, the treatment can be helpful to anyone interested in making positive and lasting changes.

This wellness planner is intended to be a helpful tool to use as you work toward building a healthier and more meaningful life using your DBT skills. You can use it to keep track of your emotions and behaviors while monitoring your progress toward your recovery goals. It's also designed to start on any date, so you can begin right away.

Remember: There is no substitute for working with a licensed mental health professional. This planner is not intended to take the place of an adherent dialectical behavior therapy treatment program.

For a complete list of skills, please see the second edition of Marsha Linehan's *DBT Skills Training Handouts and Worksheets*. This book is published by The Guilford Press and is listed in the resource section at the end of this planner.

If you find that you like DBT as much as I do, I'd love to hear from you. Please feel free to contact me at amanda@mydialecticallife.com.

Above all else, don't ever give up.

MINDFULNESS

Mindfulness is at the very heart of dialectical behavior therapy. Sometimes people think that mindfulness may refer to a mysterious spiritual or religious practice but mindfulness is really just about the way we pay attention to something on purpose and in the present moment.

Within DBT, there is an emphasis on everyday mindfulness rather than a formal meditative practice that you might be more familiar with. That means that we can be mindful while we do things like eat a piece of chocolate, drive to work, study for an important exam, talk to a friend, brush our teeth, or make our beds in the morning. We can be mindful about anything in our world.

We can also be mindful about our inner experience. That means that we might pay attention to our thoughts and emotions with a commitment to openness and curiosity. We are practicing what Buddhism refers to as "beginner's mind." When we're practicing mindfulness, it's important that we notice and then make a skillful choice to let go of judgments about ourselves and others because those judgments may cloud our ability to understand things as they truly are. Getting caught up in judgments is definitely not a part of a life worth living.

Since mindfulness is the core of DBT, we want to strive to practice all of the other skills mindfully, too. For instance, if you decide to help yourself get through a rough afternoon by using distress tolerance skills, you don't want to be watching a funny cat video while making cupcakes and thinking about the argument that happened earlier in the day. Try to slow things down by focusing on using just one skill at a time.

There's lots of important scientific evidence to suggest that regular mindfulness practice may significantly reduce symptoms related to stress and anxiety. Even two or three minutes of mindful breathing or breath counting can make a big difference in how you are feeling emotionally. In my own life, I noticed that my racing mind began to slow down to a more reasonable speed once I started to practice mindfulness a little each day. It didn't take me long to see results and I bet that you might also find that's true for you.

If you're interested in learning more about mindfulness, I can highly recommend books by Jon Kabat-Zinn. You can find several of his books listed in the resource section at the end of this planner.

DISTRESS TOLERANCE

All of us have at least some stress woven into our daily lives. Even people who don't have lots of challenges when it comes to coping with their thoughts and emotions must find ways to successfully manage everyday distress.

Dialectical behavior therapy gives us a lot of different ways to help distract and soothe ourselves when we are face-to-face with those stressful moments in our lives.

Because we're all so different, Marsha Linehan has given us many ideas to use in tolerating our distress. I use distress tolerance skills like activities, thoughts, sensations, meaning, prayer, and radical acceptance every single day. I also love to self-soothe with touch and scent. Using these skills regularly helps me to be the very best that I can be.

I hope if you haven't yet developed your own list of favorite skills, that this planner can be a tool that helps you to understand what is most beneficial to you and why.

Ideally, you'll want to make a list of skills you can use before you need them. Many of my clients find that it's helpful to make a list of things that they can do instead of engaging in self-destructive or self-defeating behaviors. Your own ideas may include things like:

- Singing loudly
- Completing a jigsaw puzzle with more than 50 pieces
- Taking funny pictures with your cell phone camera and sending them to friends
- Practicing yoga poses

- Changing the sheets on your bed
- Lighting a candle
- Writing a poem
- Mindfully describing a thought or emotion
- Working with clay

Because we all have to tolerate some stress in our day, making distress tolerance skills a priority may help you to stay emotionally regulated for longer periods of time.

One of the important keys to using distress tolerance skills is not to use them when we can solve the problem that is causing us to feel discouraged, hopeless, scared, sad, or angry. That may mean that we use other skills to help us solve the problem, ask for help, talk about what is bothering us, or take other steps to help ourselves.

A life worth living isn't a life that's spent engaging in distress tolerance from morning to night.

As with all things in life, we need balance.

EMOTION REGULATION

This is a set of skills that can help you to manage your emotions—even intense emotions—more effectively.

One of the first things you'll want to do when you feel like doing something that may make life more difficult is to stop and figure out exactly what emotion you're experiencing. Is it sadness, fear, disgust, anger, envy, hopelessness, or shame? Simply being aware of what we are feeling can be a great way to help begin to manage the intensity of the emotion. Keeping a list of emotions handy may be helpful if you have a difficult time putting a name to your feelings.

Next, you may want to decide if you want to take action to lower the intensity of a particular emotion. Often it can feel energizing to keep an emotion going. Some people feel more alive, creative, or powerful when they are experiencing an emotion very strongly. It can be almost an intoxicating experience that may sometimes lead us down the path of making decisions that make our lives even more complicated.

It's important to remember that intense emotions don't stay at the same level of intensity for long. An emotion may begin to rise in intensity like a big wave and then slowly come back down. We can help ourselves by deciding we won't react to a particular emotion until its intensity has dramatically decreased.

For example, we may notice that we have an urge to yell when we are feeling angry but that urge will begin to dissipate the longer we refrain from acting out on those emotions. Temporarily walking away from a heated argument or counting to ten before speaking really can make a difference in expertly riding out a big wave.

We can also reduce our vulnerability to experiencing intense emotions by taking care of our physical selves. For you, that may mean eating small balanced meals throughout the day, getting enough sleep, exercising daily, treating illnesses early, and refraining from self-medicating with drugs and alcohol.

Another way we can help ourselves regulate our emotions is to create situations that make us feel more of the emotions we want to feel like happiness, joy, hopefulness, love, pride, and playfulness. An important part of our emotional health means taking the time to engage in relaxing and enjoyable activities each day to increase these desired emotions.

INTERPERSONAL EFFECTIVENESS

Dialectical behavior therapy's interpersonal effectiveness skills can help us to get along better with others while also keeping—and sometimes enhancing—our own self-worth when it comes to our relationships.

For instance, sometimes people who are suffering emotionally have a challenging time asking for any kind of help. If this sounds familiar, you might also be in the habit of telling yourself that your close friends and family members should already know what you want or need before you even have to ask. What you may not know is that at times everyone needs a little assistance in asking for the things that will help us to build a life worth living.

These skills can also help you build healthier relationships in your life. Perhaps your recovery goals include having more friends that you can meet for an occasional movie or coffee, getting along better with your boss so that you're in a good position to finally ask for that raise, or maybe you want to be able to talk to that difficult person in your life without always getting into an argument or apologizing over something that may have happened years ago.

If any of these situations sound familiar, the interpersonal effectiveness skills are definitely something you'll want to integrate into your daily life.

Mastery of this set of skills may also help you to:

- Listen more effectively when talking to a friend
- Be exceptionally brave and tell the truth when it matters the most
- Show others how much you care
- Say no when a friend asks you for yet another favor

- Stand up for your own values and beliefs
- Ask for help before things become a crisis or emergency
- Negotiate to create a win-win situation

I believe that the key to successfully using these skills is to start practicing with the people in your life who don't judge you and who love you just the way you are today. Implementing interpersonal effectiveness skills with emotionally safer people can help you to take a bolder step and use these skills with those in our lives that may be demanding, exasperating, or who may also be suffering.

In essence, we are walking mindfully and slowly before we start to run that relational marathon.

SELF-CARE ASSESSMENT

Creating a life worth living when you are an emotionally sensitive person can be challenging.

Making a commitment to daily self-care can help to alleviate some of the fear, sadness, loneliness, and discouragement you might be experiencing.

Let's get started by taking the Self-Care Assessment in the next two pages.

SELF-CARE ASSESSMENT

Over the past 28 days, how often have you engaged in these specific self-care methods?

SCORING

4	Always
3	Often
2	Sometimes
1	Rarely
0	Not applicable to me at this time

PHYSICAL CARE	SCORE
Ate small balanced meals throughout the day	
Exercised for at least 15-20 minutes each day	
Followed preventive care instructions	
Bathed and brushed teeth daily	
Balanced sleep	
Refrained from self-medicating with alcohol, drugs, or prescription medicine	
Treated illness promptly	

TOTAL SCORE FOR THIS SECTION ☐

EMOTIONAL CARE	SCORE
Attended all scheduled treatment and therapy appointments	
Made time for hobbies and enjoyable activities	
Politely said no to unwanted requests	
Let others know when I needed extra help	
Spent time with friends and loved ones	
Validated my own emotions, thoughts, and experiences	
Practiced self-compassion	

TOTAL SCORE FOR THIS SECTION ☐

TOTAL SCORE PER SECTION

20-28	**Excellent!** You're doing a great job of taking care of yourself in this area.
11-19	**Very good.** Identify and address any gaps in self-care.
Below 10	**No one is perfect.** Is this an area of growth for you?

Remember, a score of zero (not applicable) in any area may lower your section score.

RELATIONAL CARE	SCORE
Stayed connected to friends and family members	
Set aside time to spend with people I care about	
Told people close to me that they were important	
Apologized or made repairs when I was wrong	
Expressed appreciation and thankfulness to others	
Empathized with others or thought about problems from their perspective	
Established limits and boundaries when necessary	

TOTAL SCORE FOR THIS SECTION

SPIRITUAL CARE	SCORE
Attended religious or spiritual services	
Spent time with others who share similar beliefs	
Sought spiritual direction or guidance	
Prayed or asked someone to pray for me	
Practiced mindfulness and/or meditation	
Identified important values and sought meaning in my life	
Read or watched things that helped to inspire me	

TOTAL SCORE FOR THIS SECTION

HOW TO USE THIS WELLNESS PLANNER

You can use this planner to make notes about the skills you are using each day, write down reminders about appointments and important events, and track your progress in treatment.

For some readers, it might be tempting to seek some kind of dialectical behavior therapy perfection. The path to recovery won't be found by doing everything right the first time you try. Over the next year you'll begin to see a pattern about what kinds of DBT skills are most helpful to you and when. If you skip a day or even a week, that's okay. Starting over again is also a very skillful behavior.

Remember to also celebrate your small successes. This is exceptionally important and hard work that you're doing. You can get started on any date. Let's begin!

First: Complete the Self-Care Assessment on pages 20 and 21, if you haven't already.

Daily: Turn the following page and start using the Daily Self-Care Tracker every day.

Monthly: Complete the Self-Care Assessment every four weeks.

Be brave as you move forward in this new life!

YOUR
DAILY
WELLNESS
PLANNER

THE WEEK AHEAD

Daily self-care tracker

		M	T	W	T	F	S	S
PHYSICAL	Exercised for at least 10–15 minutes	✓/✗						
	Took prescribed medications as directed							
	Refrained from self-medicating							
	Got enough sleep							
	Ate balanced meals							
EMOTIONAL	Skillfully tolerated distressing moments							
	Validated my own thoughts, emotions, and experiences							
	Practiced self-compassion							
	Engaged in mindful breathing or breath counting							
	Observed and described feelings mindfully							
RELATIONAL	Practiced empathy and unconditional kindness							
	Let go of judgments about others							
	Used problem-solving skills to strengthen relationships							
	Said no and established limits when necessary							
	Expressed a mindful interest in others							
SPIRITUAL	Used prayer or meditation to help myself							
	Sought or created meaning in my life							
	Allowed myself to be inspired or to inspire others							
	Honored my values and beliefs							
	Attended religious or spiritual services							

MONDAY

DATE   /   /

Skills practiced

MINDFULNESS	EMOTION REGULATION	DISTRESS TOLERANCE	INTERPERSONAL EFFECTIVENESS

Things that I'm **thankful** for

1.

2.

3.

Goals I worked towards

Today's **shining moment**

Notes and reminders

DAYS SOBER	BEHAVIOR	DAYS SINCE
OR NUMBER OF DAYS SINCE ENGAGING IN A HARMFUL OR DESTRUCTIVE BEHAVIOR		

TUESDAY

DATE / /

Skills practiced

MINDFULNESS	EMOTION REGULATION	DISTRESS TOLERANCE	INTERPERSONAL EFFECTIVENESS

Things that I'm **thankful** for

1.
2.
3.

Goals I worked towards

Today's **shining moment**

Notes and reminders

DAYS SOBER OR NUMBER OF DAYS SINCE ENGAGING IN A HARMFUL OR DESTRUCTIVE BEHAVIOR	BEHAVIOR	DAYS SINCE

WEDNESDAY

DATE / /

Skills practiced

MINDFULNESS	EMOTION REGULATION	DISTRESS TOLERANCE	INTERPERSONAL EFFECTIVENESS

Things that I'm **thankful** for

1.
2.
3.

Goals I worked towards

Today's **shining moment**

Notes and reminders

DAYS SOBER OR NUMBER OF DAYS SINCE ENGAGING IN A HARMFUL OR DESTRUCTIVE BEHAVIOR	BEHAVIOR	DAYS SINCE

THURSDAY

DATE / /

Skills practiced

MINDFULNESS	EMOTION REGULATION	DISTRESS TOLERANCE	INTERPERSONAL EFFECTIVENESS

Things that I'm **thankful** for

1.
2.
3.

Goals I worked towards

Today's **shining moment**

Notes and reminders

DAYS SOBER OR NUMBER OF DAYS SINCE ENGAGING IN A HARMFUL OR DESTRUCTIVE BEHAVIOR

BEHAVIOR	DAYS SINCE

FRIDAY

DATE / /

Skills practiced

MINDFULNESS	EMOTION REGULATION	DISTRESS TOLERANCE	INTERPERSONAL EFFECTIVENESS

Things that I'm **thankful** for

1.
2.
3.

Goals I worked towards

Today's **shining moment**

Notes and reminders

DAYS SOBER OR NUMBER OF DAYS SINCE ENGAGING IN A HARMFUL OR DESTRUCTIVE BEHAVIOR

BEHAVIOR	DAYS SINCE

SATURDAY

DATE / /

Skills practiced

MINDFULNESS	EMOTION REGULATION	DISTRESS TOLERANCE	INTERPERSONAL EFFECTIVENESS

Things that I'm **thankful** for

1.
2.
3.

Goals I worked towards

Today's **shining moment**

Notes and reminders

DAYS SOBER
OR NUMBER OF DAYS SINCE ENGAGING IN A HARMFUL OR DESTRUCTIVE BEHAVIOR

BEHAVIOR	DAYS SINCE

SUNDAY

DATE / /

Skills practiced

MINDFULNESS	EMOTION REGULATION	DISTRESS TOLERANCE	INTERPERSONAL EFFECTIVENESS

Things that I'm **thankful** for

1.
2.
3.

Goals I worked towards

Today's **shining moment**

Notes and reminders

DAYS SOBER
OR NUMBER OF DAYS SINCE ENGAGING IN A HARMFUL OR DESTRUCTIVE BEHAVIOR

BEHAVIOR	DAYS SINCE

THE WEEK AHEAD

Daily self-care tracker

		M	T	W	T	F	S	S
PHYSICAL	Exercised for at least 10-15 minutes							
	Took prescribed medications as directed							
	Refrained from self-medicating							
	Got enough sleep							
	Ate balanced meals							
EMOTIONAL	Skillfully tolerated distressing moments							
	Validated my own thoughts, emotions, and experiences							
	Practiced self-compassion							
	Engaged in mindful breathing or breath counting							
	Observed and described feelings mindfully							
RELATIONAL	Practiced empathy and unconditional kindness							
	Let go of judgments about others							
	Used problem-solving skills to strengthen relationships							
	Said no and established limits when necessary							
	Expressed a mindful interest in others							
SPIRITUAL	Used prayer or meditation to help myself							
	Sought or created meaning in my life							
	Allowed myself to be inspired or to inspire others							
	Honored my values and beliefs							
	Attended religious or spiritual services							

MONDAY

DATE   /   /

Skills practiced

MINDFULNESS	EMOTION REGULATION	DISTRESS TOLERANCE	INTERPERSONAL EFFECTIVENESS

Things that I'm **thankful** for

1.

2.

3.

Goals I worked towards

Today's **shining moment**

Notes and reminders

DAYS SOBER

OR NUMBER OF DAYS SINCE ENGAGING IN A HARMFUL OR DESTRUCTIVE BEHAVIOR

BEHAVIOR	DAYS SINCE

TUESDAY

Skills practiced

MINDFULNESS	EMOTION REGULATION	DISTRESS TOLERANCE	INTERPERSONAL EFFECTIVENESS

Things that I'm **thankful** for

1.
2.
3.

Goals I worked towards

Today's **shining moment**

Notes and reminders

DAYS SOBER OR NUMBER OF DAYS SINCE ENGAGING IN A HARMFUL OR DESTRUCTIVE BEHAVIOR	BEHAVIOR	DAYS SINCE

WEDNESDAY

Skills practiced

MINDFULNESS	EMOTION REGULATION	DISTRESS TOLERANCE	INTERPERSONAL EFFECTIVENESS

Things that I'm **thankful** for

1.
2.
3.

Goals I worked towards

Today's **shining moment**

Notes and reminders

DAYS SOBER OR NUMBER OF DAYS SINCE ENGAGING IN A HARMFUL OR DESTRUCTIVE BEHAVIOR	BEHAVIOR	DAYS SINCE

THURSDAY

Skills practiced

MINDFULNESS	EMOTION REGULATION	DISTRESS TOLERANCE	INTERPERSONAL EFFECTIVENESS

Things that I'm **thankful** for

1.
2.
3.

Goals I worked towards

Today's **shining moment**

Notes and reminders

DAYS SOBER OR NUMBER OF DAYS SINCE ENGAGING IN A HARMFUL OR DESTRUCTIVE BEHAVIOR	BEHAVIOR	DAYS SINCE
		☐ ☐ ☐
		☐ ☐ ☐
		☐ ☐ ☐

FRIDAY

DATE   /   /

Skills practiced

MINDFULNESS	EMOTION REGULATION	DISTRESS TOLERANCE	INTERPERSONAL EFFECTIVENESS

Things that I'm **thankful** for

1.
2.
3.

Goals I worked towards

Today's **shining moment**

Notes and reminders

DAYS SOBER OR NUMBER OF DAYS SINCE ENGAGING IN A HARMFUL OR DESTRUCTIVE BEHAVIOR	BEHAVIOR	DAYS SINCE
		☐ ☐ ☐
		☐ ☐ ☐
		☐ ☐ ☐

SATURDAY

Skills practiced

MINDFULNESS	EMOTION REGULATION	DISTRESS TOLERANCE	INTERPERSONAL EFFECTIVENESS

Things that I'm **thankful** for

1.
2.
3.

Goals I worked towards

Today's **shining moment**

Notes and reminders

DAYS SOBER OR NUMBER OF DAYS SINCE ENGAGING IN A HARMFUL OR DESTRUCTIVE BEHAVIOR

BEHAVIOR	DAYS SINCE

SUNDAY

DATE   /   /

Skills practiced

MINDFULNESS	EMOTION REGULATION	DISTRESS TOLERANCE	INTERPERSONAL EFFECTIVENESS

Things that I'm **thankful** for

1.
2.
3.

Goals I worked towards

Today's **shining moment**

Notes and reminders

DAYS SOBER OR NUMBER OF DAYS SINCE ENGAGING IN A HARMFUL OR DESTRUCTIVE BEHAVIOR

BEHAVIOR	DAYS SINCE

THE WEEK AHEAD

Daily self-care tracker

		M	T	W	T	F	S	S
PHYSICAL	Exercised for at least 10–15 minutes	✓						
	Took prescribed medications as directed	✗						
	Refrained from self-medicating							
	Got enough sleep							
	Ate balanced meals							
EMOTIONAL	Skillfully tolerated distressing moments							
	Validated my own thoughts, emotions, and experiences							
	Practiced self-compassion							
	Engaged in mindful breathing or breath counting							
	Observed and described feelings mindfully							
RELATIONAL	Practiced empathy and unconditional kindness							
	Let go of judgments about others							
	Used problem-solving skills to strengthen relationships							
	Said no and established limits when necessary							
	Expressed a mindful interest in others							
SPIRITUAL	Used prayer or meditation to help myself							
	Sought or created meaning in my life							
	Allowed myself to be inspired or to inspire others							
	Honored my values and beliefs							
	Attended religious or spiritual services							

MONDAY

DATE   /   /

Skills practiced

MINDFULNESS	EMOTION REGULATION	DISTRESS TOLERANCE	INTERPERSONAL EFFECTIVENESS

Things that I'm **thankful** for

1.
2.
3.

Goals I worked towards

Today's **shining moment**

Notes and reminders

DAYS SOBER
OR NUMBER OF DAYS SINCE ENGAGING IN A HARMFUL OR DESTRUCTIVE BEHAVIOR

BEHAVIOR	DAYS SINCE

TUESDAY

Skills practiced

MINDFULNESS	EMOTION REGULATION	DISTRESS TOLERANCE	INTERPERSONAL EFFECTIVENESS

Things that I'm **thankful** for

1.
2.
3.

Goals I worked towards

Today's **shining moment**

Notes and reminders

DAYS SOBER
OR NUMBER OF DAYS SINCE ENGAGING IN A HARMFUL OR DESTRUCTIVE BEHAVIOR

BEHAVIOR	DAYS SINCE

WEDNESDAY

DATE / /

Skills practiced

MINDFULNESS	EMOTION REGULATION	DISTRESS TOLERANCE	INTERPERSONAL EFFECTIVENESS

Things that I'm **thankful** for

1.
2.
3.

Goals I worked towards

Today's **shining moment**

Notes and reminders

DAYS SOBER
OR NUMBER OF DAYS SINCE ENGAGING IN A HARMFUL OR DESTRUCTIVE BEHAVIOR

BEHAVIOR	DAYS SINCE

THURSDAY

DATE / /

Skills practiced

MINDFULNESS	EMOTION REGULATION	DISTRESS TOLERANCE	INTERPERSONAL EFFECTIVENESS

Things that I'm **thankful** for

1.
2.
3.

Goals I worked towards

Today's **shining moment**

Notes and reminders

DAYS SOBER
OR NUMBER OF DAYS SINCE ENGAGING IN A HARMFUL OR DESTRUCTIVE BEHAVIOR

BEHAVIOR	DAYS SINCE

FRIDAY

DATE / /

Skills practiced

MINDFULNESS	EMOTION REGULATION	DISTRESS TOLERANCE	INTERPERSONAL EFFECTIVENESS

Things that I'm **thankful** for

1.
2.
3.

Goals I worked towards

Today's **shining moment**

Notes and reminders

DAYS SOBER
OR NUMBER OF DAYS SINCE ENGAGING IN A HARMFUL OR DESTRUCTIVE BEHAVIOR

BEHAVIOR	DAYS SINCE

SATURDAY

DATE / /

Skills practiced

MINDFULNESS	EMOTION REGULATION	DISTRESS TOLERANCE	INTERPERSONAL EFFECTIVENESS

Things that I'm **thankful** for

1.
2.
3.

Goals I worked towards

Today's **shining moment**

Notes and reminders

DAYS SOBER OR NUMBER OF DAYS SINCE ENGAGING IN A HARMFUL OR DESTRUCTIVE BEHAVIOR

BEHAVIOR	DAYS SINCE

SUNDAY

DATE / /

Skills practiced

MINDFULNESS	EMOTION REGULATION	DISTRESS TOLERANCE	INTERPERSONAL EFFECTIVENESS

Things that I'm **thankful** for

1.
2.
3.

Goals I worked towards

Today's **shining moment**

Notes and reminders

DAYS SOBER OR NUMBER OF DAYS SINCE ENGAGING IN A HARMFUL OR DESTRUCTIVE BEHAVIOR

BEHAVIOR	DAYS SINCE

THE WEEK AHEAD

Daily self-care tracker

		M	T	W	T	F	S	S
PHYSICAL	Exercised for at least 10–15 minutes	✓	✗					
	Took prescribed medications as directed							
	Refrained from self-medicating							
	Got enough sleep							
	Ate balanced meals							
EMOTIONAL	Skillfully tolerated distressing moments							
	Validated my own thoughts, emotions, and experiences							
	Practiced self-compassion							
	Engaged in mindful breathing or breath counting							
	Observed and described feelings mindfully							
RELATIONAL	Practiced empathy and unconditional kindness							
	Let go of judgments about others							
	Used problem-solving skills to strengthen relationships							
	Said no and established limits when necessary							
	Expressed a mindful interest in others							
SPIRITUAL	Used prayer or meditation to help myself							
	Sought or created meaning in my life							
	Allowed myself to be inspired or to inspire others							
	Honored my values and beliefs							
	Attended religious or spiritual services							

MONDAY

DATE   /   /

Skills practiced

MINDFULNESS	EMOTION REGULATION	DISTRESS TOLERANCE	INTERPERSONAL EFFECTIVENESS

Things that I'm **thankful** for

1.
2.
3.

Goals I worked towards

Today's **shining moment**

Notes and reminders

DAYS SOBER
OR NUMBER OF DAYS SINCE ENGAGING IN A HARMFUL OR DESTRUCTIVE BEHAVIOR

BEHAVIOR	DAYS SINCE

TUESDAY

DATE / /

Skills practiced

MINDFULNESS	EMOTION REGULATION	DISTRESS TOLERANCE	INTERPERSONAL EFFECTIVENESS

Things that I'm thankful for

1.
2.
3.

Goals I worked towards

Today's **shining moment**

Notes and reminders

DAYS SOBER OR NUMBER OF DAYS SINCE ENGAGING IN A HARMFUL OR DESTRUCTIVE BEHAVIOR	BEHAVIOR	DAYS SINCE

WEDNESDAY

DATE / /

Skills practiced

MINDFULNESS	EMOTION REGULATION	DISTRESS TOLERANCE	INTERPERSONAL EFFECTIVENESS

Things that I'm thankful for

1.
2.
3.

Goals I worked towards

Today's **shining moment**

Notes and reminders

DAYS SOBER OR NUMBER OF DAYS SINCE ENGAGING IN A HARMFUL OR DESTRUCTIVE BEHAVIOR	BEHAVIOR	DAYS SINCE

THURSDAY

DATE /   /

Skills practiced

MINDFULNESS	EMOTION REGULATION	DISTRESS TOLERANCE	INTERPERSONAL EFFECTIVENESS

Things that I'm **thankful** for

1.
2.
3.

Goals I worked towards

Today's **shining moment**

Notes and reminders

DAYS SOBER
OR NUMBER OF DAYS SINCE ENGAGING IN A HARMFUL OR DESTRUCTIVE BEHAVIOR

BEHAVIOR	DAYS SINCE

FRIDAY

DATE /   /

Skills practiced

MINDFULNESS	EMOTION REGULATION	DISTRESS TOLERANCE	INTERPERSONAL EFFECTIVENESS

Things that I'm **thankful** for

1.
2.
3.

Goals I worked towards

Today's **shining moment**

Notes and reminders

DAYS SOBER
OR NUMBER OF DAYS SINCE ENGAGING IN A HARMFUL OR DESTRUCTIVE BEHAVIOR

BEHAVIOR	DAYS SINCE

SATURDAY

DATE   /   /

Skills practiced

MINDFULNESS	EMOTION REGULATION	DISTRESS TOLERANCE	INTERPERSONAL EFFECTIVENESS

Things that I'm **thankful** for	**Goals** I worked towards	Today's **shining moment**
1.		
2.		
3.		

Notes and reminders

DAYS SOBER OR NUMBER OF DAYS SINCE ENGAGING IN A HARMFUL OR DESTRUCTIVE BEHAVIOR	BEHAVIOR	DAYS SINCE

SUNDAY

DATE   /   /

Skills practiced

MINDFULNESS	EMOTION REGULATION	DISTRESS TOLERANCE	INTERPERSONAL EFFECTIVENESS

Things that I'm **thankful** for	**Goals** I worked towards	Today's **shining moment**
1.		
2.		
3.		

Notes and reminders

DAYS SOBER OR NUMBER OF DAYS SINCE ENGAGING IN A HARMFUL OR DESTRUCTIVE BEHAVIOR	BEHAVIOR	DAYS SINCE

SELF-CARE ASSESSMENT

Over the past 28 days, how often have you engaged in these specific self-care methods?

SCORING	
4	**Always**
3	**Often**
2	**Sometimes**
1	**Rarely**
0	Not applicable to me at this time

PHYSICAL CARE	SCORE
Ate small balanced meals throughout the day	
Exercised for at least 15–20 minutes each day	
Followed preventive care instructions	
Bathed and brushed teeth daily	
Balanced sleep	
Refrained from self-medicating with alcohol, drugs, or prescription medicine	
Treated illness promptly	

TOTAL SCORE FOR THIS SECTION

EMOTIONAL CARE	SCORE
Attended all scheduled treatment and therapy appointments	
Made time for hobbies and enjoyable activities	
Politely said no to unwanted requests	
Let others know when I needed extra help	
Spent time with friends and loved ones	
Validated my own emotions, thoughts, and experiences	
Practiced self-compassion	

TOTAL SCORE FOR THIS SECTION

TOTAL SCORE PER SECTION

20-28	**Excellent!** You're doing a great job of taking care of yourself in this area.
11-19	**Very good.** Identify and address any gaps in self-care.
Below 10	**No one is perfect.** Is this an area of growth for you?

Remember, a score of zero (not applicable) in any area may lower your section score.

RELATIONAL CARE	SCORE
Stayed connected to friends and family members	
Set aside time to spend with people I care about	
Told people close to me that they were important	
Apologized or made repairs when I was wrong	
Expressed appreciation and thankfulness to others	
Empathized with others or thought about problems from their perspective	
Established limits and boundaries when necessary	

TOTAL SCORE FOR THIS SECTION

SPIRITUAL CARE	SCORE
Attended religious or spiritual services	
Spent time with others who share similar beliefs	
Sought spiritual direction or guidance	
Prayed or asked someone to pray for me	
Practiced mindfulness and/or meditation	
Identified important values and sought meaning in my life	
Read or watched things that helped to inspire me	

TOTAL SCORE FOR THIS SECTION

THE WEEK AHEAD

Daily self-care tracker

		M	T	W	T	F	S	S
PHYSICAL	Exercised for at least 10-15 minutes	✓/✗						
	Took prescribed medications as directed							
	Refrained from self-medicating							
	Got enough sleep							
	Ate balanced meals							
EMOTIONAL	Skillfully tolerated distressing moments							
	Validated my own thoughts, emotions, and experiences							
	Practiced self-compassion							
	Engaged in mindful breathing or breath counting							
	Observed and described feelings mindfully							
RELATIONAL	Practiced empathy and unconditional kindness							
	Let go of judgments about others							
	Used problem-solving skills to strengthen relationships							
	Said no and established limits when necessary							
	Expressed a mindful interest in others							
SPIRITUAL	Used prayer or meditation to help myself							
	Sought or created meaning in my life							
	Allowed myself to be inspired or to inspire others							
	Honored my values and beliefs							
	Attended religious or spiritual services							

MONDAY

DATE _____ / _____ / _____

Skills practiced

MINDFULNESS	EMOTION REGULATION	DISTRESS TOLERANCE	INTERPERSONAL EFFECTIVENESS

Things that I'm **thankful** for

1.
2.
3.

Goals I worked towards

Today's **shining moment**

Notes and reminders

DAYS SOBER
OR NUMBER OF DAYS SINCE ENGAGING IN A HARMFUL OR DESTRUCTIVE BEHAVIOR

BEHAVIOR	DAYS SINCE
	☐ ☐ ☐
	☐ ☐ ☐
	☐ ☐ ☐

TUESDAY

Skills practiced

MINDFULNESS	EMOTION REGULATION	DISTRESS TOLERANCE	INTERPERSONAL EFFECTIVENESS

Things that I'm **thankful** for

1.
2.
3.

Goals I worked towards

Today's **shining moment**

Notes and reminders

DAYS SOBER
OR NUMBER OF DAYS SINCE ENGAGING IN A HARMFUL OR DESTRUCTIVE BEHAVIOR

BEHAVIOR	DAYS SINCE

WEDNESDAY

DATE / /

Skills practiced

MINDFULNESS	EMOTION REGULATION	DISTRESS TOLERANCE	INTERPERSONAL EFFECTIVENESS

Things that I'm **thankful** for

1.
2.
3.

Goals I worked towards

Today's **shining moment**

Notes and reminders

DAYS SOBER
OR NUMBER OF DAYS SINCE ENGAGING IN A HARMFUL OR DESTRUCTIVE BEHAVIOR

BEHAVIOR	DAYS SINCE

THURSDAY

Skills practiced

MINDFULNESS	EMOTION REGULATION	DISTRESS TOLERANCE	INTERPERSONAL EFFECTIVENESS

Things that I'm **thankful** for

1.
2.
3.

Goals I worked towards

Today's **shining moment**

Notes and reminders

DAYS SOBER OR NUMBER OF DAYS SINCE ENGAGING IN A HARMFUL OR DESTRUCTIVE BEHAVIOR

BEHAVIOR	DAYS SINCE

FRIDAY

Skills practiced

MINDFULNESS	EMOTION REGULATION	DISTRESS TOLERANCE	INTERPERSONAL EFFECTIVENESS

Things that I'm **thankful** for

1.
2.
3.

Goals I worked towards

Today's **shining moment**

Notes and reminders

DAYS SOBER OR NUMBER OF DAYS SINCE ENGAGING IN A HARMFUL OR DESTRUCTIVE BEHAVIOR

BEHAVIOR	DAYS SINCE

SATURDAY

DATE / /

Skills practiced

MINDFULNESS	EMOTION REGULATION	DISTRESS TOLERANCE	INTERPERSONAL EFFECTIVENESS

Things that I'm thankful for

1.
2.
3.

Goals I worked towards

Today's shining moment

Notes and reminders

DAYS SOBER OR NUMBER OF DAYS SINCE ENGAGING IN A HARMFUL OR DESTRUCTIVE BEHAVIOR

BEHAVIOR	DAYS SINCE

SUNDAY

DATE / /

Skills practiced

MINDFULNESS	EMOTION REGULATION	DISTRESS TOLERANCE	INTERPERSONAL EFFECTIVENESS

Things that I'm thankful for

1.
2.
3.

Goals I worked towards

Today's shining moment

Notes and reminders

DAYS SOBER OR NUMBER OF DAYS SINCE ENGAGING IN A HARMFUL OR DESTRUCTIVE BEHAVIOR

BEHAVIOR	DAYS SINCE

THE WEEK AHEAD

Daily self-care tracker

		M	T	W	T	F	S	S
PHYSICAL	Exercised for at least 10-15 minutes	✓ / ✗						
	Took prescribed medications as directed							
	Refrained from self-medicating							
	Got enough sleep							
	Ate balanced meals							
EMOTIONAL	Skillfully tolerated distressing moments							
	Validated my own thoughts, emotions, and experiences							
	Practiced self-compassion							
	Engaged in mindful breathing or breath counting							
	Observed and described feelings mindfully							
RELATIONAL	Practiced empathy and unconditional kindness							
	Let go of judgments about others							
	Used problem-solving skills to strengthen relationships							
	Said no and established limits when necessary							
	Expressed a mindful interest in others							
SPIRITUAL	Used prayer or meditation to help myself							
	Sought or created meaning in my life							
	Allowed myself to be inspired or to inspire others							
	Honored my values and beliefs							
	Attended religious or spiritual services							

MONDAY

DATE   /   /

Skills practiced

MINDFULNESS	EMOTION REGULATION	DISTRESS TOLERANCE	INTERPERSONAL EFFECTIVENESS

Things that I'm **thankful** for

1.

2.

3.

Goals I worked towards

Today's **shining moment**

Notes and reminders

DAYS SOBER OR NUMBER OF DAYS SINCE ENGAGING IN A HARMFUL OR DESTRUCTIVE BEHAVIOR

BEHAVIOR	DAYS SINCE
	□ □ □
	□ □ □
	□ □ □

TUESDAY

Skills practiced

MINDFULNESS	EMOTION REGULATION	DISTRESS TOLERANCE	INTERPERSONAL EFFECTIVENESS

Things that I'm **thankful** for

1.
2.
3.

Goals I worked towards

Today's **shining moment**

Notes and reminders

DAYS SOBER
OR NUMBER OF DAYS SINCE ENGAGING IN A HARMFUL OR DESTRUCTIVE BEHAVIOR

BEHAVIOR	DAYS SINCE

WEDNESDAY

Skills practiced

MINDFULNESS	EMOTION REGULATION	DISTRESS TOLERANCE	INTERPERSONAL EFFECTIVENESS

Things that I'm **thankful** for

1.
2.
3.

Goals I worked towards

Today's **shining moment**

Notes and reminders

DAYS SOBER
OR NUMBER OF DAYS SINCE ENGAGING IN A HARMFUL OR DESTRUCTIVE BEHAVIOR

BEHAVIOR	DAYS SINCE

THURSDAY

DATE   /   /

Skills practiced

MINDFULNESS	EMOTION REGULATION	DISTRESS TOLERANCE	INTERPERSONAL EFFECTIVENESS

Things that I'm thankful for

1.
2.
3.

Goals I worked towards

Today's shining moment

Notes and reminders

DAYS SOBER OR NUMBER OF DAYS SINCE ENGAGING IN A HARMFUL OR DESTRUCTIVE BEHAVIOR	BEHAVIOR	DAYS SINCE
		☐ ☐ ☐
		☐ ☐ ☐
		☐ ☐ ☐

FRIDAY

DATE   /   /

Skills practiced

MINDFULNESS	EMOTION REGULATION	DISTRESS TOLERANCE	INTERPERSONAL EFFECTIVENESS

Things that I'm thankful for

1.
2.
3.

Goals I worked towards

Today's shining moment

Notes and reminders

DAYS SOBER OR NUMBER OF DAYS SINCE ENGAGING IN A HARMFUL OR DESTRUCTIVE BEHAVIOR	BEHAVIOR	DAYS SINCE
		☐ ☐ ☐
		☐ ☐ ☐
		☐ ☐ ☐

SATURDAY

Skills practiced

MINDFULNESS	EMOTION REGULATION	DISTRESS TOLERANCE	INTERPERSONAL EFFECTIVENESS

Things that I'm **thankful** for

1.
2.
3.

Goals I worked towards

Today's **shining moment**

Notes and reminders

DAYS SOBER OR NUMBER OF DAYS SINCE ENGAGING IN A HARMFUL OR DESTRUCTIVE BEHAVIOR	BEHAVIOR	DAYS SINCE

SUNDAY

Skills practiced

MINDFULNESS	EMOTION REGULATION	DISTRESS TOLERANCE	INTERPERSONAL EFFECTIVENESS

Things that I'm **thankful** for

1.
2.
3.

Goals I worked towards

Today's **shining moment**

Notes and reminders

DAYS SOBER OR NUMBER OF DAYS SINCE ENGAGING IN A HARMFUL OR DESTRUCTIVE BEHAVIOR	BEHAVIOR	DAYS SINCE

THE WEEK AHEAD

Daily self-care tracker

		M	T	W	T	F	S	S
PHYSICAL	Exercised for at least 10–15 minutes	✓						
	Took prescribed medications as directed	✗						
	Refrained from self-medicating							
	Got enough sleep							
	Ate balanced meals							
EMOTIONAL	Skillfully tolerated distressing moments							
	Validated my own thoughts, emotions, and experiences							
	Practiced self-compassion							
	Engaged in mindful breathing or breath counting							
	Observed and described feelings mindfully							
RELATIONAL	Practiced empathy and unconditional kindness							
	Let go of judgments about others							
	Used problem-solving skills to strengthen relationships							
	Said no and established limits when necessary							
	Expressed a mindful interest in others							
SPIRITUAL	Used prayer or meditation to help myself							
	Sought or created meaning in my life							
	Allowed myself to be inspired or to inspire others							
	Honored my values and beliefs							
	Attended religious or spiritual services							

MONDAY

DATE / /

Skills practiced

MINDFULNESS	EMOTION REGULATION	DISTRESS TOLERANCE	INTERPERSONAL EFFECTIVENESS

Things that I'm **thankful** for

1.
2.
3.

Goals I worked towards

Today's **shining moment**

Notes and reminders

DAYS SOBER
OR NUMBER OF DAYS SINCE ENGAGING IN A HARMFUL OR DESTRUCTIVE BEHAVIOR

BEHAVIOR	DAYS SINCE
	☐☐☐
	☐☐☐
	☐☐☐

TUESDAY

Skills practiced

MINDFULNESS	EMOTION REGULATION	DISTRESS TOLERANCE	INTERPERSONAL EFFECTIVENESS

Things that I'm **thankful** for

1.
2.
3.

Goals I worked towards

Today's **shining moment**

Notes and reminders

DAYS SOBER
OR NUMBER OF DAYS SINCE ENGAGING IN A HARMFUL OR DESTRUCTIVE BEHAVIOR

BEHAVIOR	DAYS SINCE

WEDNESDAY

DATE / /

Skills practiced

MINDFULNESS	EMOTION REGULATION	DISTRESS TOLERANCE	INTERPERSONAL EFFECTIVENESS

Things that I'm **thankful** for

1.
2.
3.

Goals I worked towards

Today's **shining moment**

Notes and reminders

DAYS SOBER
OR NUMBER OF DAYS SINCE ENGAGING IN A HARMFUL OR DESTRUCTIVE BEHAVIOR

BEHAVIOR	DAYS SINCE

THURSDAY

Skills practiced

MINDFULNESS	EMOTION REGULATION	DISTRESS TOLERANCE	INTERPERSONAL EFFECTIVENESS

Things that I'm **thankful** for

1.
2.
3.

Goals I worked towards

Today's **shining moment**

Notes and reminders

DAYS SOBER OR NUMBER OF DAYS SINCE ENGAGING IN A HARMFUL OR DESTRUCTIVE BEHAVIOR	BEHAVIOR	DAYS SINCE

FRIDAY

Skills practiced

MINDFULNESS	EMOTION REGULATION	DISTRESS TOLERANCE	INTERPERSONAL EFFECTIVENESS

Things that I'm **thankful** for

1.
2.
3.

Goals I worked towards

Today's **shining moment**

Notes and reminders

DAYS SOBER OR NUMBER OF DAYS SINCE ENGAGING IN A HARMFUL OR DESTRUCTIVE BEHAVIOR	BEHAVIOR	DAYS SINCE

SATURDAY

DATE / /

Skills practiced

MINDFULNESS	EMOTION REGULATION	DISTRESS TOLERANCE	INTERPERSONAL EFFECTIVENESS

Things that I'm **thankful** for

1.
2.
3.

Goals I worked towards

Today's **shining moment**

Notes and reminders

DAYS SOBER OR NUMBER OF DAYS SINCE ENGAGING IN A HARMFUL OR DESTRUCTIVE BEHAVIOR

BEHAVIOR	DAYS SINCE

SUNDAY

DATE / /

Skills practiced

MINDFULNESS	EMOTION REGULATION	DISTRESS TOLERANCE	INTERPERSONAL EFFECTIVENESS

Things that I'm **thankful** for

1.
2.
3.

Goals I worked towards

Today's **shining moment**

Notes and reminders

DAYS SOBER OR NUMBER OF DAYS SINCE ENGAGING IN A HARMFUL OR DESTRUCTIVE BEHAVIOR

BEHAVIOR	DAYS SINCE

THE WEEK AHEAD

Daily self-care tracker

		M	T	W	T	F	S	S
PHYSICAL	Exercised for at least 10–15 minutes	✓/✗						
	Took prescribed medications as directed							
	Refrained from self-medicating							
	Got enough sleep							
	Ate balanced meals							
EMOTIONAL	Skillfully tolerated distressing moments							
	Validated my own thoughts, emotions, and experiences							
	Practiced self-compassion							
	Engaged in mindful breathing or breath counting							
	Observed and described feelings mindfully							
RELATIONAL	Practiced empathy and unconditional kindness							
	Let go of judgments about others							
	Used problem-solving skills to strengthen relationships							
	Said no and established limits when necessary							
	Expressed a mindful interest in others							
SPIRITUAL	Used prayer or meditation to help myself							
	Sought or created meaning in my life							
	Allowed myself to be inspired or to inspire others							
	Honored my values and beliefs							
	Attended religious or spiritual services							

MONDAY

DATE   /   /

Skills practiced

MINDFULNESS	EMOTION REGULATION	DISTRESS TOLERANCE	INTERPERSONAL EFFECTIVENESS

Things that I'm **thankful** for

1.
2.
3.

Goals I worked towards

Today's **shining moment**

Notes and reminders

DAYS SOBER
OR NUMBER OF DAYS SINCE ENGAGING IN A HARMFUL OR DESTRUCTIVE BEHAVIOR

BEHAVIOR	DAYS SINCE

TUESDAY

DATE   /   /

Skills practiced

MINDFULNESS	EMOTION REGULATION	DISTRESS TOLERANCE	INTERPERSONAL EFFECTIVENESS

Things that I'm **thankful** for

1.
2.
3.

Goals I worked towards

Today's **shining moment**

Notes and reminders

DAYS SOBER
OR NUMBER OF DAYS SINCE ENGAGING IN A HARMFUL OR DESTRUCTIVE BEHAVIOR

BEHAVIOR	DAYS SINCE

WEDNESDAY

DATE   /   /

Skills practiced

MINDFULNESS	EMOTION REGULATION	DISTRESS TOLERANCE	INTERPERSONAL EFFECTIVENESS

Things that I'm **thankful** for

1.
2.
3.

Goals I worked towards

Today's **shining moment**

Notes and reminders

DAYS SOBER
OR NUMBER OF DAYS SINCE ENGAGING IN A HARMFUL OR DESTRUCTIVE BEHAVIOR

BEHAVIOR	DAYS SINCE

THURSDAY

Skills practiced

MINDFULNESS	EMOTION REGULATION	DISTRESS TOLERANCE	INTERPERSONAL EFFECTIVENESS

Things that I'm **thankful** for

1.
2.
3.

Goals I worked towards

Today's **shining moment**

Notes and reminders

DAYS SOBER
OR NUMBER OF DAYS SINCE ENGAGING IN A HARMFUL OR DESTRUCTIVE BEHAVIOR

BEHAVIOR	DAYS SINCE

FRIDAY

DATE   /   /

Skills practiced

MINDFULNESS	EMOTION REGULATION	DISTRESS TOLERANCE	INTERPERSONAL EFFECTIVENESS

Things that I'm **thankful** for

1.
2.
3.

Goals I worked towards

Today's **shining moment**

Notes and reminders

DAYS SOBER
OR NUMBER OF DAYS SINCE ENGAGING IN A HARMFUL OR DESTRUCTIVE BEHAVIOR

BEHAVIOR	DAYS SINCE

SATURDAY

DATE   /   /

Skills practiced

MINDFULNESS	EMOTION REGULATION	DISTRESS TOLERANCE	INTERPERSONAL EFFECTIVENESS

Things that I'm **thankful** for

1.
2.
3.

Goals I worked towards

Today's **shining moment**

Notes and reminders

DAYS SOBER
OR NUMBER OF DAYS SINCE ENGAGING IN A HARMFUL OR DESTRUCTIVE BEHAVIOR

BEHAVIOR		DAYS SINCE

SUNDAY

DATE   /   /

Skills practiced

MINDFULNESS	EMOTION REGULATION	DISTRESS TOLERANCE	INTERPERSONAL EFFECTIVENESS

Things that I'm **thankful** for

1.
2.
3.

Goals I worked towards

Today's **shining moment**

Notes and reminders

DAYS SOBER
OR NUMBER OF DAYS SINCE ENGAGING IN A HARMFUL OR DESTRUCTIVE BEHAVIOR

BEHAVIOR		DAYS SINCE

SELF-CARE ASSESSMENT

Over the past 28 days, how often have you engaged in these specific self-care methods?

PHYSICAL CARE	SCORE
Ate small balanced meals throughout the day	
Exercised for at least 15-20 minutes each day	
Followed preventive care instructions	
Bathed and brushed teeth daily	
Balanced sleep	
Refrained from self-medicating with alcohol, drugs, or prescription medicine	
Treated illness promptly	

TOTAL SCORE FOR THIS SECTION

EMOTIONAL CARE	SCORE
Attended all scheduled treatment and therapy appointments	
Made time for hobbies and enjoyable activities	
Politely said no to unwanted requests	
Let others know when I needed extra help	
Spent time with friends and loved ones	
Validated my own emotions, thoughts, and experiences	
Practiced self-compassion	

TOTAL SCORE FOR THIS SECTION

TOTAL SCORE PER SECTION

20-28	**Excellent!** You're doing a great job of taking care of yourself in this area.
11-19	**Very good.** Identify and address any gaps in self-care.
Below 10	**No one is perfect.** Is this an area of growth for you?

Remember, a score of zero (not applicable) in any area may lower your section score.

RELATIONAL CARE	SCORE
Stayed connected to friends and family members	
Set aside time to spend with people I care about	
Told people close to me that they were important	
Apologized or made repairs when I was wrong	
Expressed appreciation and thankfulness to others	
Empathized with others or thought about problems from their perspective	
Established limits and boundaries when necessary	

TOTAL SCORE FOR THIS SECTION

SPIRITUAL CARE	SCORE
Attended religious or spiritual services	
Spent time with others who share similar beliefs	
Sought spiritual direction or guidance	
Prayed or asked someone to pray for me	
Practiced mindfulness and/or meditation	
Identified important values and sought meaning in my life	
Read or watched things that helped to inspire me	

TOTAL SCORE FOR THIS SECTION

THE WEEK AHEAD

Daily self-care tracker

		M	T	W	T	F	S	S
PHYSICAL	Exercised for at least 10-15 minutes	✓/✗						
	Took prescribed medications as directed							
	Refrained from self-medicating							
	Got enough sleep							
	Ate balanced meals							
EMOTIONAL	Skillfully tolerated distressing moments							
	Validated my own thoughts, emotions, and experiences							
	Practiced self-compassion							
	Engaged in mindful breathing or breath counting							
	Observed and described feelings mindfully							
RELATIONAL	Practiced empathy and unconditional kindness							
	Let go of judgments about others							
	Used problem-solving skills to strengthen relationships							
	Said no and established limits when necessary							
	Expressed a mindful interest in others							
SPIRITUAL	Used prayer or meditation to help myself							
	Sought or created meaning in my life							
	Allowed myself to be inspired or to inspire others							
	Honored my values and beliefs							
	Attended religious or spiritual services							

MONDAY

DATE   /   /

Skills practiced

MINDFULNESS	EMOTION REGULATION	DISTRESS TOLERANCE	INTERPERSONAL EFFECTIVENESS

Things that I'm **thankful** for

1.

2.

3.

Goals I worked towards

Today's **shining moment**

Notes and reminders

DAYS SOBER	BEHAVIOR	DAYS SINCE
OR NUMBER OF DAYS SINCE ENGAGING IN A HARMFUL OR DESTRUCTIVE BEHAVIOR		

TUESDAY

DATE / /

Skills practiced

MINDFULNESS	EMOTION REGULATION	DISTRESS TOLERANCE	INTERPERSONAL EFFECTIVENESS

Things that I'm **thankful** for

1.
2.
3.

Goals I worked towards

Today's **shining moment**

Notes and reminders

DAYS SOBER OR NUMBER OF DAYS SINCE ENGAGING IN A HARMFUL OR DESTRUCTIVE BEHAVIOR

BEHAVIOR

DAYS SINCE

WEDNESDAY

DATE / /

Skills practiced

MINDFULNESS	EMOTION REGULATION	DISTRESS TOLERANCE	INTERPERSONAL EFFECTIVENESS

Things that I'm **thankful** for

1.
2.
3.

Goals I worked towards

Today's **shining moment**

Notes and reminders

DAYS SOBER OR NUMBER OF DAYS SINCE ENGAGING IN A HARMFUL OR DESTRUCTIVE BEHAVIOR

BEHAVIOR

DAYS SINCE

THURSDAY

DATE   /   /

Skills practiced

MINDFULNESS	EMOTION REGULATION	DISTRESS TOLERANCE	INTERPERSONAL EFFECTIVENESS

Things that I'm **thankful** for

1.
2.
3.

Goals I worked towards

Today's **shining moment**

Notes and reminders

DAYS SOBER
OR NUMBER OF DAYS SINCE ENGAGING IN A HARMFUL OR DESTRUCTIVE BEHAVIOR

BEHAVIOR		DAYS SINCE

FRIDAY

DATE   /   /

Skills practiced

MINDFULNESS	EMOTION REGULATION	DISTRESS TOLERANCE	INTERPERSONAL EFFECTIVENESS

Things that I'm **thankful** for

1.
2.
3.

Goals I worked towards

Today's **shining moment**

Notes and reminders

DAYS SOBER
OR NUMBER OF DAYS SINCE ENGAGING IN A HARMFUL OR DESTRUCTIVE BEHAVIOR

BEHAVIOR		DAYS SINCE

SATURDAY

Skills practiced

MINDFULNESS	EMOTION REGULATION	DISTRESS TOLERANCE	INTERPERSONAL EFFECTIVENESS

Things that I'm **thankful** for

1.
2.
3.

Goals I worked towards

Today's **shining moment**

Notes and reminders

DAYS SOBER OR NUMBER OF DAYS SINCE ENGAGING IN A HARMFUL OR DESTRUCTIVE BEHAVIOR

BEHAVIOR	DAYS SINCE

SUNDAY

Skills practiced

MINDFULNESS	EMOTION REGULATION	DISTRESS TOLERANCE	INTERPERSONAL EFFECTIVENESS

Things that I'm **thankful** for

1.
2.
3.

Goals I worked towards

Today's **shining moment**

Notes and reminders

DAYS SOBER OR NUMBER OF DAYS SINCE ENGAGING IN A HARMFUL OR DESTRUCTIVE BEHAVIOR

BEHAVIOR	DAYS SINCE

THE WEEK AHEAD

Daily self-care tracker

		M	T	W	T	F	S	S
PHYSICAL	Exercised for at least 10–15 minutes	✓						
	Took prescribed medications as directed	✗						
	Refrained from self-medicating							
	Got enough sleep							
	Ate balanced meals							
EMOTIONAL	Skillfully tolerated distressing moments							
	Validated my own thoughts, emotions, and experiences							
	Practiced self-compassion							
	Engaged in mindful breathing or breath counting							
	Observed and described feelings mindfully							
RELATIONAL	Practiced empathy and unconditional kindness							
	Let go of judgments about others							
	Used problem-solving skills to strengthen relationships							
	Said no and established limits when necessary							
	Expressed a mindful interest in others							
SPIRITUAL	Used prayer or meditation to help myself							
	Sought or created meaning in my life							
	Allowed myself to be inspired or to inspire others							
	Honored my values and beliefs							
	Attended religious or spiritual services							

MONDAY

DATE   /   /

Skills practiced

MINDFULNESS	EMOTION REGULATION	DISTRESS TOLERANCE	INTERPERSONAL EFFECTIVENESS

Things that I'm **thankful** for

1.
2.
3.

Goals I worked towards

Today's **shining moment**

Notes and reminders

DAYS SOBER
OR NUMBER OF DAYS SINCE ENGAGING IN A HARMFUL OR DESTRUCTIVE BEHAVIOR

BEHAVIOR	DAYS SINCE
	☐☐☐
	☐☐☐
	☐☐☐

TUESDAY

Skills practiced

MINDFULNESS	EMOTION REGULATION	DISTRESS TOLERANCE	INTERPERSONAL EFFECTIVENESS

Things that I'm **thankful** for

1.
2.
3.

Goals I worked towards

Today's **shining moment**

Notes and reminders

DAYS SOBER OR NUMBER OF DAYS SINCE ENGAGING IN A HARMFUL OR DESTRUCTIVE BEHAVIOR

BEHAVIOR	DAYS SINCE

WEDNESDAY

DATE / /

Skills practiced

MINDFULNESS	EMOTION REGULATION	DISTRESS TOLERANCE	INTERPERSONAL EFFECTIVENESS

Things that I'm **thankful** for

1.
2.
3.

Goals I worked towards

Today's **shining moment**

Notes and reminders

DAYS SOBER OR NUMBER OF DAYS SINCE ENGAGING IN A HARMFUL OR DESTRUCTIVE BEHAVIOR

BEHAVIOR	DAYS SINCE

THURSDAY

DATE   /   /

Skills practiced

MINDFULNESS	EMOTION REGULATION	DISTRESS TOLERANCE	INTERPERSONAL EFFECTIVENESS

Things that I'm **thankful** for

1.
2.
3.

Goals I worked towards

Today's **shining moment**

Notes and reminders

DAYS SOBER OR NUMBER OF DAYS SINCE ENGAGING IN A HARMFUL OR DESTRUCTIVE BEHAVIOR

BEHAVIOR	DAYS SINCE

FRIDAY

DATE   /   /

Skills practiced

MINDFULNESS	EMOTION REGULATION	DISTRESS TOLERANCE	INTERPERSONAL EFFECTIVENESS

Things that I'm **thankful** for

1.
2.
3.

Goals I worked towards

Today's **shining moment**

Notes and reminders

DAYS SOBER OR NUMBER OF DAYS SINCE ENGAGING IN A HARMFUL OR DESTRUCTIVE BEHAVIOR

BEHAVIOR	DAYS SINCE

SATURDAY

DATE / /

Skills practiced

MINDFULNESS	EMOTION REGULATION	DISTRESS TOLERANCE	INTERPERSONAL EFFECTIVENESS

Things that I'm **thankful** for

1.
2.
3.

Goals I worked towards

Today's **shining moment**

Notes and reminders

DAYS SOBER
OR NUMBER OF DAYS SINCE ENGAGING IN A HARMFUL OR DESTRUCTIVE BEHAVIOR

BEHAVIOR	DAYS SINCE

SUNDAY

DATE / /

Skills practiced

MINDFULNESS	EMOTION REGULATION	DISTRESS TOLERANCE	INTERPERSONAL EFFECTIVENESS

Things that I'm **thankful** for

1.
2.
3.

Goals I worked towards

Today's **shining moment**

Notes and reminders

DAYS SOBER
OR NUMBER OF DAYS SINCE ENGAGING IN A HARMFUL OR DESTRUCTIVE BEHAVIOR

BEHAVIOR	DAYS SINCE

THE WEEK AHEAD

Daily self-care tracker

		M	T	W	T	F	S	S
PHYSICAL	Exercised for at least 10–15 minutes	✓ ✗						
	Took prescribed medications as directed							
	Refrained from self-medicating							
	Got enough sleep							
	Ate balanced meals							
EMOTIONAL	Skillfully tolerated distressing moments							
	Validated my own thoughts, emotions, and experiences							
	Practiced self-compassion							
	Engaged in mindful breathing or breath counting							
	Observed and described feelings mindfully							
RELATIONAL	Practiced empathy and unconditional kindness							
	Let go of judgments about others							
	Used problem-solving skills to strengthen relationships							
	Said no and established limits when necessary							
	Expressed a mindful interest in others							
SPIRITUAL	Used prayer or meditation to help myself							
	Sought or created meaning in my life							
	Allowed myself to be inspired or to inspire others							
	Honored my values and beliefs							
	Attended religious or spiritual services							

MONDAY

DATE   /   /

Skills practiced

MINDFULNESS	EMOTION REGULATION	DISTRESS TOLERANCE	INTERPERSONAL EFFECTIVENESS

Things that I'm **thankful** for

1.
2.
3.

Goals I worked towards

Today's **shining moment**

Notes and reminders

DAYS SOBER

OR NUMBER OF DAYS SINCE ENGAGING IN A HARMFUL OR DESTRUCTIVE BEHAVIOR

BEHAVIOR	DAYS SINCE
	☐ ☐ ☐
	☐ ☐ ☐
	☐ ☐ ☐

TUESDAY

Skills practiced

MINDFULNESS	EMOTION REGULATION	DISTRESS TOLERANCE	INTERPERSONAL EFFECTIVENESS

Things that I'm thankful for

1.
2.
3.

Goals I worked towards

Today's shining moment

Notes and reminders

DAYS SOBER
OR NUMBER OF DAYS SINCE ENGAGING IN A HARMFUL OR DESTRUCTIVE BEHAVIOR

BEHAVIOR	DAYS SINCE

WEDNESDAY

Skills practiced

MINDFULNESS	EMOTION REGULATION	DISTRESS TOLERANCE	INTERPERSONAL EFFECTIVENESS

Things that I'm thankful for

1.
2.
3.

Goals I worked towards

Today's shining moment

Notes and reminders

DAYS SOBER
OR NUMBER OF DAYS SINCE ENGAGING IN A HARMFUL OR DESTRUCTIVE BEHAVIOR

BEHAVIOR	DAYS SINCE

THURSDAY

DATE / /

Skills practiced

MINDFULNESS	EMOTION REGULATION	DISTRESS TOLERANCE	INTERPERSONAL EFFECTIVENESS

Things that I'm **thankful** for

1.
2.
3.

Goals I worked towards

Today's **shining moment**

Notes and reminders

DAYS SOBER
OR NUMBER OF DAYS SINCE ENGAGING IN A HARMFUL OR DESTRUCTIVE BEHAVIOR

BEHAVIOR	DAYS SINCE

FRIDAY

DATE / /

Skills practiced

MINDFULNESS	EMOTION REGULATION	DISTRESS TOLERANCE	INTERPERSONAL EFFECTIVENESS

Things that I'm **thankful** for

1.
2.
3.

Goals I worked towards

Today's **shining moment**

Notes and reminders

DAYS SOBER
OR NUMBER OF DAYS SINCE ENGAGING IN A HARMFUL OR DESTRUCTIVE BEHAVIOR

BEHAVIOR	DAYS SINCE

SATURDAY

DATE   /   /

Skills practiced

MINDFULNESS	EMOTION REGULATION	DISTRESS TOLERANCE	INTERPERSONAL EFFECTIVENESS

Things that I'm **thankful** for

1.
2.
3.

Goals I worked towards

Today's **shining moment**

Notes and reminders

DAYS SOBER
OR NUMBER OF DAYS SINCE ENGAGING IN A HARMFUL OR DESTRUCTIVE BEHAVIOR

BEHAVIOR	DAYS SINCE

SUNDAY

DATE   /   /

Skills practiced

MINDFULNESS	EMOTION REGULATION	DISTRESS TOLERANCE	INTERPERSONAL EFFECTIVENESS

Things that I'm **thankful** for

1.
2.
3.

Goals I worked towards

Today's **shining moment**

Notes and reminders

DAYS SOBER
OR NUMBER OF DAYS SINCE ENGAGING IN A HARMFUL OR DESTRUCTIVE BEHAVIOR

BEHAVIOR	DAYS SINCE

THE WEEK AHEAD

Daily self-care tracker

		M	T	W	T	F	S	S
PHYSICAL	Exercised for at least 10-15 minutes	✓ ✗						
	Took prescribed medications as directed							
	Refrained from self-medicating							
	Got enough sleep							
	Ate balanced meals							
EMOTIONAL	Skillfully tolerated distressing moments							
	Validated my own thoughts, emotions, and experiences							
	Practiced self-compassion							
	Engaged in mindful breathing or breath counting							
	Observed and described feelings mindfully							
RELATIONAL	Practiced empathy and unconditional kindness							
	Let go of judgments about others							
	Used problem-solving skills to strengthen relationships							
	Said no and established limits when necessary							
	Expressed a mindful interest in others							
SPIRITUAL	Used prayer or meditation to help myself							
	Sought or created meaning in my life							
	Allowed myself to be inspired or to inspire others							
	Honored my values and beliefs							
	Attended religious or spiritual services							

MONDAY

DATE   /   /

Skills practiced

MINDFULNESS	EMOTION REGULATION	DISTRESS TOLERANCE	INTERPERSONAL EFFECTIVENESS

Things that I'm **thankful** for

1.
2.
3.

Goals I worked towards

Today's **shining moment**

Notes and reminders

DAYS SOBER
OR NUMBER OF DAYS SINCE ENGAGING IN A HARMFUL OR DESTRUCTIVE BEHAVIOR

BEHAVIOR	DAYS SINCE
	☐ ☐ ☐
	☐ ☐ ☐
	☐ ☐ ☐

TUESDAY

DATE / /

Skills practiced

MINDFULNESS	EMOTION REGULATION	DISTRESS TOLERANCE	INTERPERSONAL EFFECTIVENESS

Things that I'm **thankful** for

1.
2.
3.

Goals I worked towards

Today's **shining moment**

Notes and reminders

DAYS SOBER OR NUMBER OF DAYS SINCE ENGAGING IN A HARMFUL OR DESTRUCTIVE BEHAVIOR	BEHAVIOR	DAYS SINCE

WEDNESDAY

DATE / /

Skills practiced

MINDFULNESS	EMOTION REGULATION	DISTRESS TOLERANCE	INTERPERSONAL EFFECTIVENESS

Things that I'm **thankful** for

1.
2.
3.

Goals I worked towards

Today's **shining moment**

Notes and reminders

DAYS SOBER OR NUMBER OF DAYS SINCE ENGAGING IN A HARMFUL OR DESTRUCTIVE BEHAVIOR	BEHAVIOR	DAYS SINCE

THURSDAY

DATE / /

Skills practiced

MINDFULNESS	EMOTION REGULATION	DISTRESS TOLERANCE	INTERPERSONAL EFFECTIVENESS

Things that I'm **thankful** for

1.
2.
3.

Goals I worked towards

Today's **shining moment**

Notes and reminders

DAYS SOBER OR NUMBER OF DAYS SINCE ENGAGING IN A HARMFUL OR DESTRUCTIVE BEHAVIOR	BEHAVIOR	DAYS SINCE

FRIDAY

DATE / /

Skills practiced

MINDFULNESS	EMOTION REGULATION	DISTRESS TOLERANCE	INTERPERSONAL EFFECTIVENESS

Things that I'm **thankful** for

1.
2.
3.

Goals I worked towards

Today's **shining moment**

Notes and reminders

DAYS SOBER OR NUMBER OF DAYS SINCE ENGAGING IN A HARMFUL OR DESTRUCTIVE BEHAVIOR	BEHAVIOR	DAYS SINCE

SATURDAY

DATE   /   /

Skills practiced

MINDFULNESS	EMOTION REGULATION	DISTRESS TOLERANCE	INTERPERSONAL EFFECTIVENESS

Things that I'm **thankful** for

1.
2.
3.

Goals I worked towards

Today's **shining moment**

Notes and reminders

DAYS SOBER OR NUMBER OF DAYS SINCE ENGAGING IN A HARMFUL OR DESTRUCTIVE BEHAVIOR

BEHAVIOR	DAYS SINCE

SUNDAY

DATE   /   /

Skills practiced

MINDFULNESS	EMOTION REGULATION	DISTRESS TOLERANCE	INTERPERSONAL EFFECTIVENESS

Things that I'm **thankful** for

1.
2.
3.

Goals I worked towards

Today's **shining moment**

Notes and reminders

DAYS SOBER OR NUMBER OF DAYS SINCE ENGAGING IN A HARMFUL OR DESTRUCTIVE BEHAVIOR

BEHAVIOR	DAYS SINCE

SELF-CARE ASSESSMENT

Over the past 28 days, how often have you engaged in these specific self-care methods?

SCORING

4 **Always**

3 **Often**

2 **Sometimes**

1 **Rarely**

0 Not applicable to me at this time

PHYSICAL CARE	SCORE
Ate small balanced meals throughout the day	
Exercised for at least 15–20 minutes each day	
Followed preventive care instructions	
Bathed and brushed teeth daily	
Balanced sleep	
Refrained from self-medicating with alcohol, drugs, or prescription medicine	
Treated illness promptly	

TOTAL SCORE FOR THIS SECTION

EMOTIONAL CARE	SCORE
Attended all scheduled treatment and therapy appointments	
Made time for hobbies and enjoyable activities	
Politely said no to unwanted requests	
Let others know when I needed extra help	
Spent time with friends and loved ones	
Validated my own emotions, thoughts, and experiences	
Practiced self-compassion	

TOTAL SCORE FOR THIS SECTION

TOTAL SCORE PER SECTION

20-28	**Excellent!** You're doing a great job of taking care of yourself in this area.
11-19	**Very good.** Identify and address any gaps in self-care.
Below 10	**No one is perfect.** Is this an area of growth for you?

Remember, a score of zero (not applicable) in any area may lower your section score.

RELATIONAL CARE	SCORE
Stayed connected to friends and family members	
Set aside time to spend with people I care about	
Told people close to me that they were important	
Apologized or made repairs when I was wrong	
Expressed appreciation and thankfulness to others	
Empathized with others or thought about problems from their perspective	
Established limits and boundaries when necessary	

TOTAL SCORE FOR THIS SECTION

SPIRITUAL CARE	SCORE
Attended religious or spiritual services	
Spent time with others who share similar beliefs	
Sought spiritual direction or guidance	
Prayed or asked someone to pray for me	
Practiced mindfulness and/or meditation	
Identified important values and sought meaning in my life	
Read or watched things that helped to inspire me	

TOTAL SCORE FOR THIS SECTION

THE WEEK AHEAD

Daily self-care tracker

		M	T	W	T	F	S	S
PHYSICAL	Exercised for at least 10-15 minutes	✓ ✗						
	Took prescribed medications as directed							
	Refrained from self-medicating							
	Got enough sleep							
	Ate balanced meals							
EMOTIONAL	Skillfully tolerated distressing moments							
	Validated my own thoughts, emotions, and experiences							
	Practiced self-compassion							
	Engaged in mindful breathing or breath counting							
	Observed and described feelings mindfully							
RELATIONAL	Practiced empathy and unconditional kindness							
	Let go of judgments about others							
	Used problem-solving skills to strengthen relationships							
	Said no and established limits when necessary							
	Expressed a mindful interest in others							
SPIRITUAL	Used prayer or meditation to help myself							
	Sought or created meaning in my life							
	Allowed myself to be inspired or to inspire others							
	Honored my values and beliefs							
	Attended religious or spiritual services							

MONDAY

DATE ___ / ___ / ___

Skills practiced

MINDFULNESS	EMOTION REGULATION	DISTRESS TOLERANCE	INTERPERSONAL EFFECTIVENESS

Things that I'm thankful for

1.

2.

3.

Goals I worked towards

Today's **shining moment**

Notes and reminders

DAYS SOBER
OR NUMBER OF DAYS SINCE ENGAGING IN A HARMFUL OR DESTRUCTIVE BEHAVIOR

BEHAVIOR	DAYS SINCE
	☐ ☐ ☐
	☐ ☐ ☐
	☐ ☐ ☐

TUESDAY

DATE / /

Skills practiced

MINDFULNESS	EMOTION REGULATION	DISTRESS TOLERANCE	INTERPERSONAL EFFECTIVENESS

Things that I'm **thankful** for

1.
2.
3.

Goals I worked towards

Today's **shining moment**

Notes and reminders

DAYS SOBER OR NUMBER OF DAYS SINCE ENGAGING IN A HARMFUL OR DESTRUCTIVE BEHAVIOR

BEHAVIOR	DAYS SINCE

WEDNESDAY

DATE / /

Skills practiced

MINDFULNESS	EMOTION REGULATION	DISTRESS TOLERANCE	INTERPERSONAL EFFECTIVENESS

Things that I'm **thankful** for

1.
2.
3.

Goals I worked towards

Today's **shining moment**

Notes and reminders

DAYS SOBER OR NUMBER OF DAYS SINCE ENGAGING IN A HARMFUL OR DESTRUCTIVE BEHAVIOR

BEHAVIOR	DAYS SINCE

THURSDAY

DATE / /

Skills practiced

MINDFULNESS	EMOTION REGULATION	DISTRESS TOLERANCE	INTERPERSONAL EFFECTIVENESS

Things that I'm **thankful** for

1.
2.
3.

Goals I worked towards

Today's **shining moment**

Notes and reminders

DAYS SOBER
OR NUMBER OF DAYS SINCE ENGAGING IN A HARMFUL OR DESTRUCTIVE BEHAVIOR

BEHAVIOR	DAYS SINCE

FRIDAY

DATE / /

Skills practiced

MINDFULNESS	EMOTION REGULATION	DISTRESS TOLERANCE	INTERPERSONAL EFFECTIVENESS

Things that I'm **thankful** for

1.
2.
3.

Goals I worked towards

Today's **shining moment**

Notes and reminders

DAYS SOBER
OR NUMBER OF DAYS SINCE ENGAGING IN A HARMFUL OR DESTRUCTIVE BEHAVIOR

BEHAVIOR	DAYS SINCE

SATURDAY

DATE / /

Skills practiced

MINDFULNESS	EMOTION REGULATION	DISTRESS TOLERANCE	INTERPERSONAL EFFECTIVENESS

Things that I'm **thankful** for

1.
2.
3.

Goals I worked towards

Today's **shining moment**

Notes and reminders

DAYS SOBER OR NUMBER OF DAYS SINCE ENGAGING IN A HARMFUL OR DESTRUCTIVE BEHAVIOR

BEHAVIOR	DAYS SINCE

SUNDAY

DATE / /

Skills practiced

MINDFULNESS	EMOTION REGULATION	DISTRESS TOLERANCE	INTERPERSONAL EFFECTIVENESS

Things that I'm **thankful** for

1.
2.
3.

Goals I worked towards

Today's **shining moment**

Notes and reminders

DAYS SOBER OR NUMBER OF DAYS SINCE ENGAGING IN A HARMFUL OR DESTRUCTIVE BEHAVIOR

BEHAVIOR	DAYS SINCE

THE WEEK AHEAD

Daily self-care tracker

		M	T	W	T	F	S	S
PHYSICAL	Exercised for at least 10-15 minutes							
	Took prescribed medications as directed							
	Refrained from self-medicating							
	Got enough sleep							
	Ate balanced meals							
EMOTIONAL	Skillfully tolerated distressing moments							
	Validated my own thoughts, emotions, and experiences							
	Practiced self-compassion							
	Engaged in mindful breathing or breath counting							
	Observed and described feelings mindfully							
RELATIONAL	Practiced empathy and unconditional kindness							
	Let go of judgments about others							
	Used problem-solving skills to strengthen relationships							
	Said no and established limits when necessary							
	Expressed a mindful interest in others							
SPIRITUAL	Used prayer or meditation to help myself							
	Sought or created meaning in my life							
	Allowed myself to be inspired or to inspire others							
	Honored my values and beliefs							
	Attended religious or spiritual services							

MONDAY

DATE   /   /

Skills practiced

MINDFULNESS	EMOTION REGULATION	DISTRESS TOLERANCE	INTERPERSONAL EFFECTIVENESS

Things that I'm **thankful** for

1.
2.
3.

Goals I worked towards

Today's **shining moment**

Notes and reminders

DAYS SOBER OR NUMBER OF DAYS SINCE ENGAGING IN A HARMFUL OR DESTRUCTIVE BEHAVIOR

BEHAVIOR	DAYS SINCE

TUESDAY

Skills practiced

MINDFULNESS	EMOTION REGULATION	DISTRESS TOLERANCE	INTERPERSONAL EFFECTIVENESS

Things that I'm thankful for

1.
2.
3.

Goals I worked towards

Today's shining moment

Notes and reminders

DAYS SOBER	BEHAVIOR	DAYS SINCE
OR NUMBER OF DAYS SINCE ENGAGING IN A HARMFUL OR DESTRUCTIVE BEHAVIOR		

WEDNESDAY

Skills practiced

MINDFULNESS	EMOTION REGULATION	DISTRESS TOLERANCE	INTERPERSONAL EFFECTIVENESS

Things that I'm thankful for

1.
2.
3.

Goals I worked towards

Today's shining moment

Notes and reminders

DAYS SOBER	BEHAVIOR	DAYS SINCE
OR NUMBER OF DAYS SINCE ENGAGING IN A HARMFUL OR DESTRUCTIVE BEHAVIOR		

THURSDAY

Skills practiced

MINDFULNESS	EMOTION REGULATION	DISTRESS TOLERANCE	INTERPERSONAL EFFECTIVENESS

Things that I'm **thankful** for

1.
2.
3.

Goals I worked towards

Today's **shining moment**

Notes and reminders

DAYS SOBER OR NUMBER OF DAYS SINCE ENGAGING IN A HARMFUL OR DESTRUCTIVE BEHAVIOR

BEHAVIOR	DAYS SINCE

FRIDAY

Skills practiced

MINDFULNESS	EMOTION REGULATION	DISTRESS TOLERANCE	INTERPERSONAL EFFECTIVENESS

Things that I'm **thankful** for

1.
2.
3.

Goals I worked towards

Today's **shining moment**

Notes and reminders

DAYS SOBER OR NUMBER OF DAYS SINCE ENGAGING IN A HARMFUL OR DESTRUCTIVE BEHAVIOR

BEHAVIOR	DAYS SINCE

SATURDAY

Skills practiced

MINDFULNESS	EMOTION REGULATION	DISTRESS TOLERANCE	INTERPERSONAL EFFECTIVENESS

Things that I'm **thankful** for

1.
2.
3.

Goals I worked towards

Today's **shining moment**

Notes and reminders

DAYS SOBER OR NUMBER OF DAYS SINCE ENGAGING IN A HARMFUL OR DESTRUCTIVE BEHAVIOR

BEHAVIOR	DAYS SINCE

SUNDAY

DATE   /   /

Skills practiced

MINDFULNESS	EMOTION REGULATION	DISTRESS TOLERANCE	INTERPERSONAL EFFECTIVENESS

Things that I'm **thankful** for

1.
2.
3.

Goals I worked towards

Today's **shining moment**

Notes and reminders

DAYS SOBER OR NUMBER OF DAYS SINCE ENGAGING IN A HARMFUL OR DESTRUCTIVE BEHAVIOR

BEHAVIOR	DAYS SINCE

THE WEEK AHEAD

Daily self-care tracker

		M	T	W	T	F	S	S
PHYSICAL	Exercised for at least 10–15 minutes							
	Took prescribed medications as directed							
	Refrained from self-medicating							
	Got enough sleep							
	Ate balanced meals							
EMOTIONAL	Skillfully tolerated distressing moments							
	Validated my own thoughts, emotions, and experiences							
	Practiced self-compassion							
	Engaged in mindful breathing or breath counting							
	Observed and described feelings mindfully							
RELATIONAL	Practiced empathy and unconditional kindness							
	Let go of judgments about others							
	Used problem-solving skills to strengthen relationships							
	Said no and established limits when necessary							
	Expressed a mindful interest in others							
SPIRITUAL	Used prayer or meditation to help myself							
	Sought or created meaning in my life							
	Allowed myself to be inspired or to inspire others							
	Honored my values and beliefs							
	Attended religious or spiritual services							

MONDAY

DATE   /   /

Skills practiced

MINDFULNESS	EMOTION REGULATION	DISTRESS TOLERANCE	INTERPERSONAL EFFECTIVENESS

Things that I'm **thankful** for

1.
2.
3.

Goals I worked towards

Today's **shining moment**

Notes and reminders

DAYS SOBER
OR NUMBER OF DAYS SINCE ENGAGING IN A HARMFUL OR DESTRUCTIVE BEHAVIOR

BEHAVIOR	DAYS SINCE

TUESDAY

DATE   /   /

Skills practiced

MINDFULNESS	EMOTION REGULATION	DISTRESS TOLERANCE	INTERPERSONAL EFFECTIVENESS

Things that I'm **thankful** for

1.
2.
3.

Goals I worked towards

Today's **shining moment**

Notes and reminders

DAYS SOBER OR NUMBER OF DAYS SINCE ENGAGING IN A HARMFUL OR DESTRUCTIVE BEHAVIOR	BEHAVIOR	DAYS SINCE

WEDNESDAY

DATE   /   /

Skills practiced

MINDFULNESS	EMOTION REGULATION	DISTRESS TOLERANCE	INTERPERSONAL EFFECTIVENESS

Things that I'm **thankful** for

1.
2.
3.

Goals I worked towards

Today's **shining moment**

Notes and reminders

DAYS SOBER OR NUMBER OF DAYS SINCE ENGAGING IN A HARMFUL OR DESTRUCTIVE BEHAVIOR	BEHAVIOR	DAYS SINCE

THURSDAY

Skills practiced

MINDFULNESS	EMOTION REGULATION	DISTRESS TOLERANCE	INTERPERSONAL EFFECTIVENESS

Things that I'm **thankful** for

1.
2.
3.

Goals I worked towards

Today's **shining moment**

Notes and reminders

DAYS SOBER OR NUMBER OF DAYS SINCE ENGAGING IN A HARMFUL OR DESTRUCTIVE BEHAVIOR

BEHAVIOR	DAYS SINCE

FRIDAY

DATE   /   /

Skills practiced

MINDFULNESS	EMOTION REGULATION	DISTRESS TOLERANCE	INTERPERSONAL EFFECTIVENESS

Things that I'm **thankful** for

1.
2.
3.

Goals I worked towards

Today's **shining moment**

Notes and reminders

DAYS SOBER OR NUMBER OF DAYS SINCE ENGAGING IN A HARMFUL OR DESTRUCTIVE BEHAVIOR

BEHAVIOR	DAYS SINCE

SATURDAY

Skills practiced

MINDFULNESS	EMOTION REGULATION	DISTRESS TOLERANCE	INTERPERSONAL EFFECTIVENESS

Things that I'm **thankful** for

1.
2.
3.

Goals I worked towards

Today's **shining moment**

Notes and reminders

DAYS SOBER OR NUMBER OF DAYS SINCE ENGAGING IN A HARMFUL OR DESTRUCTIVE BEHAVIOR	BEHAVIOR	DAYS SINCE

SUNDAY

Skills practiced

MINDFULNESS	EMOTION REGULATION	DISTRESS TOLERANCE	INTERPERSONAL EFFECTIVENESS

Things that I'm **thankful** for

1.
2.
3.

Goals I worked towards

Today's **shining moment**

Notes and reminders

DAYS SOBER OR NUMBER OF DAYS SINCE ENGAGING IN A HARMFUL OR DESTRUCTIVE BEHAVIOR	BEHAVIOR	DAYS SINCE

THE WEEK AHEAD

Daily self-care tracker

		M	T	W	T	F	S	S
PHYSICAL	Exercised for at least 10-15 minutes	✓						
	Took prescribed medications as directed	✗						
	Refrained from self-medicating							
	Got enough sleep							
	Ate balanced meals							
EMOTIONAL	Skillfully tolerated distressing moments							
	Validated my own thoughts, emotions, and experiences							
	Practiced self-compassion							
	Engaged in mindful breathing or breath counting							
	Observed and described feelings mindfully							
RELATIONAL	Practiced empathy and unconditional kindness							
	Let go of judgments about others							
	Used problem-solving skills to strengthen relationships							
	Said no and established limits when necessary							
	Expressed a mindful interest in others							
SPIRITUAL	Used prayer or meditation to help myself							
	Sought or created meaning in my life							
	Allowed myself to be inspired or to inspire others							
	Honored my values and beliefs							
	Attended religious or spiritual services							

MONDAY

DATE   /   /

Skills practiced

MINDFULNESS	EMOTION REGULATION	DISTRESS TOLERANCE	INTERPERSONAL EFFECTIVENESS

Things that I'm **thankful** for

1.
2.
3.

Goals I worked towards

Today's **shining moment**

Notes and reminders

DAYS SOBER

OR NUMBER OF DAYS SINCE ENGAGING IN A HARMFUL OR DESTRUCTIVE BEHAVIOR

BEHAVIOR	DAYS SINCE

TUESDAY

DATE   /   /

Skills practiced

MINDFULNESS	EMOTION REGULATION	DISTRESS TOLERANCE	INTERPERSONAL EFFECTIVENESS

Things that I'm **thankful** for

1.
2.
3.

Goals I worked towards

Today's **shining moment**

Notes and reminders

DAYS SOBER
OR NUMBER OF DAYS SINCE ENGAGING IN A HARMFUL OR DESTRUCTIVE BEHAVIOR

BEHAVIOR	DAYS SINCE

WEDNESDAY

DATE   /   /

Skills practiced

MINDFULNESS	EMOTION REGULATION	DISTRESS TOLERANCE	INTERPERSONAL EFFECTIVENESS

Things that I'm **thankful** for

1.
2.
3.

Goals I worked towards

Today's **shining moment**

Notes and reminders

DAYS SOBER
OR NUMBER OF DAYS SINCE ENGAGING IN A HARMFUL OR DESTRUCTIVE BEHAVIOR

BEHAVIOR	DAYS SINCE

THURSDAY

Skills practiced

MINDFULNESS	EMOTION REGULATION	DISTRESS TOLERANCE	INTERPERSONAL EFFECTIVENESS

Things that I'm **thankful** for

1.
2.
3.

Goals I worked towards

Today's **shining moment**

Notes and reminders

DAYS SOBER
OR NUMBER OF DAYS SINCE ENGAGING IN A HARMFUL OR DESTRUCTIVE BEHAVIOR

BEHAVIOR	DAYS SINCE

FRIDAY

Skills practiced

MINDFULNESS	EMOTION REGULATION	DISTRESS TOLERANCE	INTERPERSONAL EFFECTIVENESS

Things that I'm **thankful** for

1.
2.
3.

Goals I worked towards

Today's **shining moment**

Notes and reminders

DAYS SOBER
OR NUMBER OF DAYS SINCE ENGAGING IN A HARMFUL OR DESTRUCTIVE BEHAVIOR

BEHAVIOR	DAYS SINCE

SATURDAY

DATE / /

Skills practiced

MINDFULNESS	EMOTION REGULATION	DISTRESS TOLERANCE	INTERPERSONAL EFFECTIVENESS

Things that I'm **thankful** for

1.
2.
3.

Goals I worked towards

Today's **shining moment**

Notes and reminders

DAYS SOBER OR NUMBER OF DAYS SINCE ENGAGING IN A HARMFUL OR DESTRUCTIVE BEHAVIOR	BEHAVIOR	DAYS SINCE

SUNDAY

DATE / /

Skills practiced

MINDFULNESS	EMOTION REGULATION	DISTRESS TOLERANCE	INTERPERSONAL EFFECTIVENESS

Things that I'm **thankful** for

1.
2.
3.

Goals I worked towards

Today's **shining moment**

Notes and reminders

DAYS SOBER OR NUMBER OF DAYS SINCE ENGAGING IN A HARMFUL OR DESTRUCTIVE BEHAVIOR	BEHAVIOR	DAYS SINCE

SELF-CARE ASSESSMENT

Over the past 28 days, how often have you engaged in these specific self-care methods?

SCORING

4	**Always**
3	**Often**
2	**Sometimes**
1	**Rarely**
0	Not applicable to me at this time

PHYSICAL CARE	SCORE
Ate small balanced meals throughout the day	
Exercised for at least 15–20 minutes each day	
Followed preventive care instructions	
Bathed and brushed teeth daily	
Balanced sleep	
Refrained from self-medicating with alcohol, drugs, or prescription medicine	
Treated illness promptly	

TOTAL SCORE FOR THIS SECTION

EMOTIONAL CARE	SCORE
Attended all scheduled treatment and therapy appointments	
Made time for hobbies and enjoyable activities	
Politely said no to unwanted requests	
Let others know when I needed extra help	
Spent time with friends and loved ones	
Validated my own emotions, thoughts, and experiences	
Practiced self-compassion	

TOTAL SCORE FOR THIS SECTION

TOTAL SCORE PER SECTION

20-28	**Excellent!** You're doing a great job of taking care of yourself in this area.
11-19	**Very good.** Identify and address any gaps in self-care.
Below 10	**No one is perfect.** Is this an area of growth for you?

Remember, a score of zero (not applicable) in any area may lower your section score.

RELATIONAL CARE	SCORE
Stayed connected to friends and family members	
Set aside time to spend with people I care about	
Told people close to me that they were important	
Apologized or made repairs when I was wrong	
Expressed appreciation and thankfulness to others	
Empathized with others or thought about problems from their perspective	
Established limits and boundaries when necessary	

TOTAL SCORE FOR THIS SECTION

SPIRITUAL CARE	SCORE
Attended religious or spiritual services	
Spent time with others who share similar beliefs	
Sought spiritual direction or guidance	
Prayed or asked someone to pray for me	
Practiced mindfulness and/or meditation	
Identified important values and sought meaning in my life	
Read or watched things that helped to inspire me	

TOTAL SCORE FOR THIS SECTION

THE WEEK AHEAD

Daily self-care tracker

		M	T	W	T	F	S	S
PHYSICAL	Exercised for at least 10-15 minutes	✓ ✗						
	Took prescribed medications as directed							
	Refrained from self-medicating							
	Got enough sleep							
	Ate balanced meals							
EMOTIONAL	Skillfully tolerated distressing moments							
	Validated my own thoughts, emotions, and experiences							
	Practiced self-compassion							
	Engaged in mindful breathing or breath counting							
	Observed and described feelings mindfully							
RELATIONAL	Practiced empathy and unconditional kindness							
	Let go of judgments about others							
	Used problem-solving skills to strengthen relationships							
	Said no and established limits when necessary							
	Expressed a mindful interest in others							
SPIRITUAL	Used prayer or meditation to help myself							
	Sought or created meaning in my life							
	Allowed myself to be inspired or to inspire others							
	Honored my values and beliefs							
	Attended religious or spiritual services							

MONDAY

DATE   /   /

Skills practiced

MINDFULNESS	EMOTION REGULATION	DISTRESS TOLERANCE	INTERPERSONAL EFFECTIVENESS

Things that I'm **thankful** for

1.
2.
3.

Goals I worked towards

Today's **shining moment**

Notes and reminders

DAYS SOBER
OR NUMBER OF DAYS SINCE ENGAGING IN A HARMFUL OR DESTRUCTIVE BEHAVIOR

BEHAVIOR	DAYS SINCE
	☐ ☐ ☐
	☐ ☐ ☐
	☐ ☐ ☐

TUESDAY

DATE   /   /

Skills practiced

MINDFULNESS	EMOTION REGULATION	DISTRESS TOLERANCE	INTERPERSONAL EFFECTIVENESS

Things that I'm **thankful** for

1.
2.
3.

Goals I worked towards

Today's **shining moment**

Notes and reminders

DAYS SOBER OR NUMBER OF DAYS SINCE ENGAGING IN A HARMFUL OR DESTRUCTIVE BEHAVIOR	BEHAVIOR	DAYS SINCE

WEDNESDAY

DATE   /   /

Skills practiced

MINDFULNESS	EMOTION REGULATION	DISTRESS TOLERANCE	INTERPERSONAL EFFECTIVENESS

Things that I'm **thankful** for

1.
2.
3.

Goals I worked towards

Today's **shining moment**

Notes and reminders

DAYS SOBER OR NUMBER OF DAYS SINCE ENGAGING IN A HARMFUL OR DESTRUCTIVE BEHAVIOR	BEHAVIOR	DAYS SINCE

THURSDAY

Skills practiced

MINDFULNESS	EMOTION REGULATION	DISTRESS TOLERANCE	INTERPERSONAL EFFECTIVENESS

Things that I'm **thankful** for

1.
2.
3.

Goals I worked towards

Today's **shining moment**

Notes and reminders

DAYS SOBER OR NUMBER OF DAYS SINCE ENGAGING IN A HARMFUL OR DESTRUCTIVE BEHAVIOR

BEHAVIOR	DAYS SINCE

FRIDAY

Skills practiced

MINDFULNESS	EMOTION REGULATION	DISTRESS TOLERANCE	INTERPERSONAL EFFECTIVENESS

Things that I'm **thankful** for

1.
2.
3.

Goals I worked towards

Today's **shining moment**

Notes and reminders

DAYS SOBER OR NUMBER OF DAYS SINCE ENGAGING IN A HARMFUL OR DESTRUCTIVE BEHAVIOR

BEHAVIOR	DAYS SINCE

SATURDAY

DATE / /

Skills practiced

MINDFULNESS	EMOTION REGULATION	DISTRESS TOLERANCE	INTERPERSONAL EFFECTIVENESS

Things that I'm **thankful** for

1.
2.
3.

Goals I worked towards

Today's **shining moment**

Notes and reminders

DAYS SOBER OR NUMBER OF DAYS SINCE ENGAGING IN A HARMFUL OR DESTRUCTIVE BEHAVIOR

BEHAVIOR	DAYS SINCE

SUNDAY

DATE / /

Skills practiced

MINDFULNESS	EMOTION REGULATION	DISTRESS TOLERANCE	INTERPERSONAL EFFECTIVENESS

Things that I'm **thankful** for

1.
2.
3.

Goals I worked towards

Today's **shining moment**

Notes and reminders

DAYS SOBER OR NUMBER OF DAYS SINCE ENGAGING IN A HARMFUL OR DESTRUCTIVE BEHAVIOR

BEHAVIOR	DAYS SINCE

THE WEEK AHEAD

Daily self-care tracker

		M	T	W	T	F	S	S
PHYSICAL	Exercised for at least 10–15 minutes	✓/✗						
	Took prescribed medications as directed							
	Refrained from self-medicating							
	Got enough sleep							
	Ate balanced meals							
EMOTIONAL	Skillfully tolerated distressing moments							
	Validated my own thoughts, emotions, and experiences							
	Practiced self-compassion							
	Engaged in mindful breathing or breath counting							
	Observed and described feelings mindfully							
RELATIONAL	Practiced empathy and unconditional kindness							
	Let go of judgments about others							
	Used problem-solving skills to strengthen relationships							
	Said no and established limits when necessary							
	Expressed a mindful interest in others							
SPIRITUAL	Used prayer or meditation to help myself							
	Sought or created meaning in my life							
	Allowed myself to be inspired or to inspire others							
	Honored my values and beliefs							
	Attended religious or spiritual services							

MONDAY

DATE / /

Skills practiced

MINDFULNESS	EMOTION REGULATION	DISTRESS TOLERANCE	INTERPERSONAL EFFECTIVENESS

Things that I'm **thankful** for

1.
2.
3.

Goals I worked towards

Today's **shining moment**

Notes and reminders

DAYS SOBER
OR NUMBER OF DAYS SINCE ENGAGING IN A HARMFUL OR DESTRUCTIVE BEHAVIOR

BEHAVIOR	DAYS SINCE

TUESDAY

DATE / /

Skills practiced

MINDFULNESS	EMOTION REGULATION	DISTRESS TOLERANCE	INTERPERSONAL EFFECTIVENESS

Things that I'm **thankful** for

1.
2.
3.

Goals I worked towards

Today's **shining moment**

Notes and reminders

DAYS SOBER
OR NUMBER OF DAYS SINCE ENGAGING IN A HARMFUL OR DESTRUCTIVE BEHAVIOR

BEHAVIOR	DAYS SINCE

WEDNESDAY

DATE / /

Skills practiced

MINDFULNESS	EMOTION REGULATION	DISTRESS TOLERANCE	INTERPERSONAL EFFECTIVENESS

Things that I'm **thankful** for

1.
2.
3.

Goals I worked towards

Today's **shining moment**

Notes and reminders

DAYS SOBER
OR NUMBER OF DAYS SINCE ENGAGING IN A HARMFUL OR DESTRUCTIVE BEHAVIOR

BEHAVIOR	DAYS SINCE

THURSDAY

DATE   /   /

Skills practiced

MINDFULNESS	EMOTION REGULATION	DISTRESS TOLERANCE	INTERPERSONAL EFFECTIVENESS

Things that I'm **thankful** for

1.
2.
3.

Goals I worked towards

Today's **shining moment**

Notes and reminders

DAYS SOBER
OR NUMBER OF DAYS SINCE ENGAGING IN A HARMFUL OR DESTRUCTIVE BEHAVIOR

BEHAVIOR	DAYS SINCE

FRIDAY

DATE   /   /

Skills practiced

MINDFULNESS	EMOTION REGULATION	DISTRESS TOLERANCE	INTERPERSONAL EFFECTIVENESS

Things that I'm **thankful** for

1.
2.
3.

Goals I worked towards

Today's **shining moment**

Notes and reminders

DAYS SOBER
OR NUMBER OF DAYS SINCE ENGAGING IN A HARMFUL OR DESTRUCTIVE BEHAVIOR

BEHAVIOR	DAYS SINCE

SATURDAY

Skills practiced

MINDFULNESS	EMOTION REGULATION	DISTRESS TOLERANCE	INTERPERSONAL EFFECTIVENESS

Things that I'm **thankful** for

1.
2.
3.

Goals I worked towards

Today's **shining moment**

Notes and reminders

DAYS SOBER
OR NUMBER OF DAYS SINCE ENGAGING IN A HARMFUL OR DESTRUCTIVE BEHAVIOR

BEHAVIOR	DAYS SINCE

SUNDAY

DATE / /

Skills practiced

MINDFULNESS	EMOTION REGULATION	DISTRESS TOLERANCE	INTERPERSONAL EFFECTIVENESS

Things that I'm **thankful** for

1.
2.
3.

Goals I worked towards

Today's **shining moment**

Notes and reminders

DAYS SOBER
OR NUMBER OF DAYS SINCE ENGAGING IN A HARMFUL OR DESTRUCTIVE BEHAVIOR

BEHAVIOR	DAYS SINCE

THE WEEK AHEAD

Daily self-care tracker

		M	T	W	T	F	S	S
PHYSICAL	Exercised for at least 10–15 minutes	✓/✗						
	Took prescribed medications as directed							
	Refrained from self-medicating							
	Got enough sleep							
	Ate balanced meals							
EMOTIONAL	Skillfully tolerated distressing moments							
	Validated my own thoughts, emotions, and experiences							
	Practiced self-compassion							
	Engaged in mindful breathing or breath counting							
	Observed and described feelings mindfully							
RELATIONAL	Practiced empathy and unconditional kindness							
	Let go of judgments about others							
	Used problem-solving skills to strengthen relationships							
	Said no and established limits when necessary							
	Expressed a mindful interest in others							
SPIRITUAL	Used prayer or meditation to help myself							
	Sought or created meaning in my life							
	Allowed myself to be inspired or to inspire others							
	Honored my values and beliefs							
	Attended religious or spiritual services							

MONDAY

DATE   /   /

Skills practiced

MINDFULNESS	EMOTION REGULATION	DISTRESS TOLERANCE	INTERPERSONAL EFFECTIVENESS

Things that I'm **thankful** for

1.
2.
3.

Goals I worked towards

Today's **shining moment**

Notes and reminders

DAYS SOBER
OR NUMBER OF DAYS SINCE ENGAGING IN A HARMFUL OR DESTRUCTIVE BEHAVIOR

BEHAVIOR	DAYS SINCE

TUESDAY

Skills practiced

MINDFULNESS	EMOTION REGULATION	DISTRESS TOLERANCE	INTERPERSONAL EFFECTIVENESS

Things that I'm **thankful** for

1.
2.
3.

Goals I worked towards

Today's **shining moment**

Notes and reminders

DAYS SOBER
OR NUMBER OF DAYS SINCE ENGAGING IN A HARMFUL OR DESTRUCTIVE BEHAVIOR

BEHAVIOR	DAYS SINCE

WEDNESDAY

Skills practiced

MINDFULNESS	EMOTION REGULATION	DISTRESS TOLERANCE	INTERPERSONAL EFFECTIVENESS

Things that I'm **thankful** for

1.
2.
3.

Goals I worked towards

Today's **shining moment**

Notes and reminders

DAYS SOBER
OR NUMBER OF DAYS SINCE ENGAGING IN A HARMFUL OR DESTRUCTIVE BEHAVIOR

BEHAVIOR	DAYS SINCE

THURSDAY

Skills practiced

MINDFULNESS	EMOTION REGULATION	DISTRESS TOLERANCE	INTERPERSONAL EFFECTIVENESS

Things that I'm **thankful** for

1.
2.
3.

Goals I worked towards

Today's **shining moment**

Notes and reminders

DAYS SOBER
OR NUMBER OF DAYS SINCE ENGAGING IN A HARMFUL OR DESTRUCTIVE BEHAVIOR

BEHAVIOR	DAYS SINCE

FRIDAY

Skills practiced

MINDFULNESS	EMOTION REGULATION	DISTRESS TOLERANCE	INTERPERSONAL EFFECTIVENESS

Things that I'm **thankful** for

1.
2.
3.

Goals I worked towards

Today's **shining moment**

Notes and reminders

DAYS SOBER
OR NUMBER OF DAYS SINCE ENGAGING IN A HARMFUL OR DESTRUCTIVE BEHAVIOR

BEHAVIOR	DAYS SINCE

SATURDAY

DATE / /

Skills practiced

MINDFULNESS	EMOTION REGULATION	DISTRESS TOLERANCE	INTERPERSONAL EFFECTIVENESS

Things that I'm **thankful** for

1.
2.
3.

Goals I worked towards

Today's **shining moment**

Notes and reminders

DAYS SOBER OR NUMBER OF DAYS SINCE ENGAGING IN A HARMFUL OR DESTRUCTIVE BEHAVIOR

BEHAVIOR	DAYS SINCE

SUNDAY

DATE / /

Skills practiced

MINDFULNESS	EMOTION REGULATION	DISTRESS TOLERANCE	INTERPERSONAL EFFECTIVENESS

Things that I'm **thankful** for

1.
2.
3.

Goals I worked towards

Today's **shining moment**

Notes and reminders

DAYS SOBER OR NUMBER OF DAYS SINCE ENGAGING IN A HARMFUL OR DESTRUCTIVE BEHAVIOR

BEHAVIOR	DAYS SINCE

THE WEEK AHEAD

Daily self-care tracker

		M	T	W	T	F	S	S
PHYSICAL	Exercised for at least 10-15 minutes	✓						
	Took prescribed medications as directed	✗						
	Refrained from self-medicating							
	Got enough sleep							
	Ate balanced meals							
EMOTIONAL	Skillfully tolerated distressing moments							
	Validated my own thoughts, emotions, and experiences							
	Practiced self-compassion							
	Engaged in mindful breathing or breath counting							
	Observed and described feelings mindfully							
RELATIONAL	Practiced empathy and unconditional kindness							
	Let go of judgments about others							
	Used problem-solving skills to strengthen relationships							
	Said no and established limits when necessary							
	Expressed a mindful interest in others							
SPIRITUAL	Used prayer or meditation to help myself							
	Sought or created meaning in my life							
	Allowed myself to be inspired or to inspire others							
	Honored my values and beliefs							
	Attended religious or spiritual services							

MONDAY

DATE   /   /

Skills practiced

MINDFULNESS	EMOTION REGULATION	DISTRESS TOLERANCE	INTERPERSONAL EFFECTIVENESS

Things that I'm **thankful** for

1.
2.
3.

Goals I worked towards

Today's **shining moment**

Notes and reminders

DAYS SOBER

OR NUMBER OF DAYS SINCE ENGAGING IN A HARMFUL OR DESTRUCTIVE BEHAVIOR

BEHAVIOR	DAYS SINCE

TUESDAY

DATE   /   /

Skills practiced

MINDFULNESS	EMOTION REGULATION	DISTRESS TOLERANCE	INTERPERSONAL EFFECTIVENESS

Things that I'm thankful for

1.
2.
3.

Goals I worked towards

Today's shining moment

Notes and reminders

DAYS SOBER
OR NUMBER OF DAYS SINCE ENGAGING IN A HARMFUL OR DESTRUCTIVE BEHAVIOR

BEHAVIOR	DAYS SINCE

WEDNESDAY

DATE   /   /

Skills practiced

MINDFULNESS	EMOTION REGULATION	DISTRESS TOLERANCE	INTERPERSONAL EFFECTIVENESS

Things that I'm thankful for

1.
2.
3.

Goals I worked towards

Today's shining moment

Notes and reminders

DAYS SOBER
OR NUMBER OF DAYS SINCE ENGAGING IN A HARMFUL OR DESTRUCTIVE BEHAVIOR

BEHAVIOR	DAYS SINCE

THURSDAY

Skills practiced

MINDFULNESS	EMOTION REGULATION	DISTRESS TOLERANCE	INTERPERSONAL EFFECTIVENESS

Things that I'm **thankful** for

1.
2.
3.

Goals I worked towards

Today's **shining moment**

Notes and reminders

DAYS SOBER
OR NUMBER OF DAYS SINCE ENGAGING IN A HARMFUL OR DESTRUCTIVE BEHAVIOR

BEHAVIOR	DAYS SINCE

FRIDAY

DATE / /

Skills practiced

MINDFULNESS	EMOTION REGULATION	DISTRESS TOLERANCE	INTERPERSONAL EFFECTIVENESS

Things that I'm **thankful** for

1.
2.
3.

Goals I worked towards

Today's **shining moment**

Notes and reminders

DAYS SOBER
OR NUMBER OF DAYS SINCE ENGAGING IN A HARMFUL OR DESTRUCTIVE BEHAVIOR

BEHAVIOR	DAYS SINCE

SATURDAY

DATE   /   /

Skills practiced

MINDFULNESS	EMOTION REGULATION	DISTRESS TOLERANCE	INTERPERSONAL EFFECTIVENESS

Things that I'm **thankful** for

1.
2.
3.

Goals I worked towards

Today's **shining moment**

Notes and reminders

DAYS SOBER OR NUMBER OF DAYS SINCE ENGAGING IN A HARMFUL OR DESTRUCTIVE BEHAVIOR

BEHAVIOR	DAYS SINCE

SUNDAY

DATE   /   /

Skills practiced

MINDFULNESS	EMOTION REGULATION	DISTRESS TOLERANCE	INTERPERSONAL EFFECTIVENESS

Things that I'm **thankful** for

1.
2.
3.

Goals I worked towards

Today's **shining moment**

Notes and reminders

DAYS SOBER OR NUMBER OF DAYS SINCE ENGAGING IN A HARMFUL OR DESTRUCTIVE BEHAVIOR

BEHAVIOR	DAYS SINCE

SELF-CARE ASSESSMENT

Over the past 28 days, how often have you engaged in these specific self-care methods?

PHYSICAL CARE	SCORE
Ate small balanced meals throughout the day	
Exercised for at least 15-20 minutes each day	
Followed preventive care instructions	
Bathed and brushed teeth daily	
Balanced sleep	
Refrained from self-medicating with alcohol, drugs, or prescription medicine	
Treated illness promptly	

TOTAL SCORE FOR THIS SECTION

EMOTIONAL CARE	SCORE
Attended all scheduled treatment and therapy appointments	
Made time for hobbies and enjoyable activities	
Politely said no to unwanted requests	
Let others know when I needed extra help	
Spent time with friends and loved ones	
Validated my own emotions, thoughts, and experiences	
Practiced self-compassion	

TOTAL SCORE FOR THIS SECTION

TOTAL SCORE PER SECTION

20-28	**Excellent!** You're doing a great job of taking care of yourself in this area.
11-19	**Very good.** Identify and address any gaps in self-care.
Below 10	**No one is perfect.** Is this an area of growth for you?

Remember, a score of zero (not applicable) in any area may lower your section score.

RELATIONAL CARE	SCORE
Stayed connected to friends and family members	
Set aside time to spend with people I care about	
Told people close to me that they were important	
Apologized or made repairs when I was wrong	
Expressed appreciation and thankfulness to others	
Empathized with others or thought about problems from their perspective	
Established limits and boundaries when necessary	

TOTAL SCORE FOR THIS SECTION

SPIRITUAL CARE	SCORE
Attended religious or spiritual services	
Spent time with others who share similar beliefs	
Sought spiritual direction or guidance	
Prayed or asked someone to pray for me	
Practiced mindfulness and/or meditation	
Identified important values and sought meaning in my life	
Read or watched things that helped to inspire me	

TOTAL SCORE FOR THIS SECTION

THE WEEK AHEAD

Daily self-care tracker

		M	T	W	T	F	S	S
PHYSICAL	Exercised for at least 10-15 minutes	✓						
	Took prescribed medications as directed	✗						
	Refrained from self-medicating							
	Got enough sleep							
	Ate balanced meals							
EMOTIONAL	Skillfully tolerated distressing moments							
	Validated my own thoughts, emotions, and experiences							
	Practiced self-compassion							
	Engaged in mindful breathing or breath counting							
	Observed and described feelings mindfully							
RELATIONAL	Practiced empathy and unconditional kindness							
	Let go of judgments about others							
	Used problem-solving skills to strengthen relationships							
	Said no and established limits when necessary							
	Expressed a mindful interest in others							
SPIRITUAL	Used prayer or meditation to help myself							
	Sought or created meaning in my life							
	Allowed myself to be inspired or to inspire others							
	Honored my values and beliefs							
	Attended religious or spiritual services							

MONDAY

DATE   /   /

Skills practiced

MINDFULNESS	EMOTION REGULATION	DISTRESS TOLERANCE	INTERPERSONAL EFFECTIVENESS

Things that I'm **thankful** for

1.

2.

3.

Goals I worked towards

Today's **shining moment**

Notes and reminders

DAYS SOBER OR NUMBER OF DAYS SINCE ENGAGING IN A HARMFUL OR DESTRUCTIVE BEHAVIOR	BEHAVIOR	DAYS SINCE
		☐ ☐ ☐
		☐ ☐ ☐
		☐ ☐ ☐

TUESDAY

DATE / /

Skills practiced

MINDFULNESS	EMOTION REGULATION	DISTRESS TOLERANCE	INTERPERSONAL EFFECTIVENESS

Things that I'm **thankful** for

1.
2.
3.

Goals I worked towards

Today's **shining moment**

Notes and reminders

DAYS SOBER OR NUMBER OF DAYS SINCE ENGAGING IN A HARMFUL OR DESTRUCTIVE BEHAVIOR

BEHAVIOR	DAYS SINCE

WEDNESDAY

DATE / /

Skills practiced

MINDFULNESS	EMOTION REGULATION	DISTRESS TOLERANCE	INTERPERSONAL EFFECTIVENESS

Things that I'm **thankful** for

1.
2.
3.

Goals I worked towards

Today's **shining moment**

Notes and reminders

DAYS SOBER OR NUMBER OF DAYS SINCE ENGAGING IN A HARMFUL OR DESTRUCTIVE BEHAVIOR

BEHAVIOR	DAYS SINCE

THURSDAY

Skills practiced

MINDFULNESS	EMOTION REGULATION	DISTRESS TOLERANCE	INTERPERSONAL EFFECTIVENESS

Things that I'm **thankful** for

1.
2.
3.

Goals I worked towards

Today's **shining moment**

Notes and reminders

DAYS SOBER OR NUMBER OF DAYS SINCE ENGAGING IN A HARMFUL OR DESTRUCTIVE BEHAVIOR

BEHAVIOR	DAYS SINCE

FRIDAY

Skills practiced

MINDFULNESS	EMOTION REGULATION	DISTRESS TOLERANCE	INTERPERSONAL EFFECTIVENESS

Things that I'm **thankful** for

1.
2.
3.

Goals I worked towards

Today's **shining moment**

Notes and reminders

DAYS SOBER OR NUMBER OF DAYS SINCE ENGAGING IN A HARMFUL OR DESTRUCTIVE BEHAVIOR

BEHAVIOR	DAYS SINCE

SATURDAY

DATE / /

Skills practiced

MINDFULNESS	EMOTION REGULATION	DISTRESS TOLERANCE	INTERPERSONAL EFFECTIVENESS

Things that I'm **thankful** for

1.
2.
3.

Goals I worked towards

Today's **shining moment**

Notes and reminders

DAYS SOBER OR NUMBER OF DAYS SINCE ENGAGING IN A HARMFUL OR DESTRUCTIVE BEHAVIOR

BEHAVIOR	DAYS SINCE

SUNDAY

DATE / /

Skills practiced

MINDFULNESS	EMOTION REGULATION	DISTRESS TOLERANCE	INTERPERSONAL EFFECTIVENESS

Things that I'm **thankful** for

1.
2.
3.

Goals I worked towards

Today's **shining moment**

Notes and reminders

DAYS SOBER OR NUMBER OF DAYS SINCE ENGAGING IN A HARMFUL OR DESTRUCTIVE BEHAVIOR

BEHAVIOR	DAYS SINCE

THE WEEK AHEAD

Daily self-care tracker

		M	T	W	T	F	S	S
PHYSICAL	Exercised for at least 10-15 minutes	✓/✗						
	Took prescribed medications as directed							
	Refrained from self-medicating							
	Got enough sleep							
	Ate balanced meals							
EMOTIONAL	Skillfully tolerated distressing moments							
	Validated my own thoughts, emotions, and experiences							
	Practiced self-compassion							
	Engaged in mindful breathing or breath counting							
	Observed and described feelings mindfully							
RELATIONAL	Practiced empathy and unconditional kindness							
	Let go of judgments about others							
	Used problem-solving skills to strengthen relationships							
	Said no and established limits when necessary							
	Expressed a mindful interest in others							
SPIRITUAL	Used prayer or meditation to help myself							
	Sought or created meaning in my life							
	Allowed myself to be inspired or to inspire others							
	Honored my values and beliefs							
	Attended religious or spiritual services							

MONDAY

DATE / /

Skills practiced

MINDFULNESS	EMOTION REGULATION	DISTRESS TOLERANCE	INTERPERSONAL EFFECTIVENESS

Things that I'm **thankful** for

1.
2.
3.

Goals I worked towards

Today's **shining moment**

Notes and reminders

DAYS SOBER
OR NUMBER OF DAYS SINCE ENGAGING IN A HARMFUL OR DESTRUCTIVE BEHAVIOR

BEHAVIOR	DAYS SINCE
	☐☐☐
	☐☐☐
	☐☐☐

TUESDAY

Skills practiced

MINDFULNESS	EMOTION REGULATION	DISTRESS TOLERANCE	INTERPERSONAL EFFECTIVENESS

Things that I'm thankful for

1.
2.
3.

Goals I worked towards

Today's **shining moment**

Notes and reminders

DAYS SOBER OR NUMBER OF DAYS SINCE ENGAGING IN A HARMFUL OR DESTRUCTIVE BEHAVIOR	BEHAVIOR	DAYS SINCE

WEDNESDAY

DATE / /

Skills practiced

MINDFULNESS	EMOTION REGULATION	DISTRESS TOLERANCE	INTERPERSONAL EFFECTIVENESS

Things that I'm thankful for

1.
2.
3.

Goals I worked towards

Today's **shining moment**

Notes and reminders

DAYS SOBER OR NUMBER OF DAYS SINCE ENGAGING IN A HARMFUL OR DESTRUCTIVE BEHAVIOR	BEHAVIOR	DAYS SINCE

THURSDAY

Skills practiced

MINDFULNESS	EMOTION REGULATION	DISTRESS TOLERANCE	INTERPERSONAL EFFECTIVENESS

Things that I'm **thankful** for

1.

2.

3.

Goals I worked towards

Today's **shining moment**

Notes and reminders

DAYS SOBER
OR NUMBER OF DAYS SINCE ENGAGING IN A HARMFUL OR DESTRUCTIVE BEHAVIOR

BEHAVIOR	DAYS SINCE

FRIDAY

DATE   /   /

Skills practiced

MINDFULNESS	EMOTION REGULATION	DISTRESS TOLERANCE	INTERPERSONAL EFFECTIVENESS

Things that I'm **thankful** for

1.

2.

3.

Goals I worked towards

Today's **shining moment**

Notes and reminders

DAYS SOBER
OR NUMBER OF DAYS SINCE ENGAGING IN A HARMFUL OR DESTRUCTIVE BEHAVIOR

BEHAVIOR	DAYS SINCE

SATURDAY

DATE   /   /

Skills practiced

MINDFULNESS	EMOTION REGULATION	DISTRESS TOLERANCE	INTERPERSONAL EFFECTIVENESS

Things that I'm **thankful** for

1.
2.
3.

Goals I worked towards

Today's **shining moment**

Notes and reminders

DAYS SOBER
OR NUMBER OF DAYS SINCE ENGAGING IN A HARMFUL OR DESTRUCTIVE BEHAVIOR

BEHAVIOR	DAYS SINCE

SUNDAY

DATE   /   /

Skills practiced

MINDFULNESS	EMOTION REGULATION	DISTRESS TOLERANCE	INTERPERSONAL EFFECTIVENESS

Things that I'm **thankful** for

1.
2.
3.

Goals I worked towards

Today's **shining moment**

Notes and reminders

DAYS SOBER
OR NUMBER OF DAYS SINCE ENGAGING IN A HARMFUL OR DESTRUCTIVE BEHAVIOR

BEHAVIOR	DAYS SINCE

THE WEEK AHEAD

Daily self-care tracker

		M	T	W	T	F	S	S
PHYSICAL	Exercised for at least 10-15 minutes	✓/✗						
	Took prescribed medications as directed							
	Refrained from self-medicating							
	Got enough sleep							
	Ate balanced meals							
EMOTIONAL	Skillfully tolerated distressing moments							
	Validated my own thoughts, emotions, and experiences							
	Practiced self-compassion							
	Engaged in mindful breathing or breath counting							
	Observed and described feelings mindfully							
RELATIONAL	Practiced empathy and unconditional kindness							
	Let go of judgments about others							
	Used problem-solving skills to strengthen relationships							
	Said no and established limits when necessary							
	Expressed a mindful interest in others							
SPIRITUAL	Used prayer or meditation to help myself							
	Sought or created meaning in my life							
	Allowed myself to be inspired or to inspire others							
	Honored my values and beliefs							
	Attended religious or spiritual services							

MONDAY

DATE   /   /

Skills practiced

MINDFULNESS	EMOTION REGULATION	DISTRESS TOLERANCE	INTERPERSONAL EFFECTIVENESS

Things that I'm **thankful** for

1.
2.
3.

Goals I worked towards

Today's **shining moment**

Notes and reminders

DAYS SOBER
OR NUMBER OF DAYS SINCE ENGAGING IN A HARMFUL OR DESTRUCTIVE BEHAVIOR

BEHAVIOR	DAYS SINCE
	☐☐☐
	☐☐☐
	☐☐☐

TUESDAY

DATE   /   /

Skills practiced

MINDFULNESS	EMOTION REGULATION	DISTRESS TOLERANCE	INTERPERSONAL EFFECTIVENESS

Things that I'm **thankful** for

1.
2.
3.

Goals I worked towards

Today's **shining moment**

Notes and reminders

DAYS SOBER
OR NUMBER OF DAYS SINCE ENGAGING IN A HARMFUL OR DESTRUCTIVE BEHAVIOR

BEHAVIOR	DAYS SINCE

WEDNESDAY

DATE   /   /

Skills practiced

MINDFULNESS	EMOTION REGULATION	DISTRESS TOLERANCE	INTERPERSONAL EFFECTIVENESS

Things that I'm **thankful** for

1.
2.
3.

Goals I worked towards

Today's **shining moment**

Notes and reminders

DAYS SOBER
OR NUMBER OF DAYS SINCE ENGAGING IN A HARMFUL OR DESTRUCTIVE BEHAVIOR

BEHAVIOR	DAYS SINCE

THURSDAY

Skills practiced

MINDFULNESS	EMOTION REGULATION	DISTRESS TOLERANCE	INTERPERSONAL EFFECTIVENESS

Things that I'm **thankful** for

1.
2.
3.

Goals I worked towards

Today's **shining moment**

Notes and reminders

DAYS SOBER OR NUMBER OF DAYS SINCE ENGAGING IN A HARMFUL OR DESTRUCTIVE BEHAVIOR

BEHAVIOR	DAYS SINCE

FRIDAY

DATE / /

Skills practiced

MINDFULNESS	EMOTION REGULATION	DISTRESS TOLERANCE	INTERPERSONAL EFFECTIVENESS

Things that I'm **thankful** for

1.
2.
3.

Goals I worked towards

Today's **shining moment**

Notes and reminders

DAYS SOBER OR NUMBER OF DAYS SINCE ENGAGING IN A HARMFUL OR DESTRUCTIVE BEHAVIOR

BEHAVIOR	DAYS SINCE

SATURDAY

DATE / /

Skills practiced

MINDFULNESS	EMOTION REGULATION	DISTRESS TOLERANCE	INTERPERSONAL EFFECTIVENESS

Things that I'm **thankful** for

1.
2.
3.

Goals I worked towards

Today's **shining moment**

Notes and reminders

DAYS SOBER OR NUMBER OF DAYS SINCE ENGAGING IN A HARMFUL OR DESTRUCTIVE BEHAVIOR

BEHAVIOR

DAYS SINCE

SUNDAY

DATE / /

Skills practiced

MINDFULNESS	EMOTION REGULATION	DISTRESS TOLERANCE	INTERPERSONAL EFFECTIVENESS

Things that I'm **thankful** for

1.
2.
3.

Goals I worked towards

Today's **shining moment**

Notes and reminders

DAYS SOBER OR NUMBER OF DAYS SINCE ENGAGING IN A HARMFUL OR DESTRUCTIVE BEHAVIOR

BEHAVIOR

DAYS SINCE

THE WEEK AHEAD

Daily self-care tracker

		M	T	W	T	F	S	S
PHYSICAL	Exercised for at least 10-15 minutes	✓✗						
	Took prescribed medications as directed							
	Refrained from self-medicating							
	Got enough sleep							
	Ate balanced meals							
EMOTIONAL	Skillfully tolerated distressing moments							
	Validated my own thoughts, emotions, and experiences							
	Practiced self-compassion							
	Engaged in mindful breathing or breath counting							
	Observed and described feelings mindfully							
RELATIONAL	Practiced empathy and unconditional kindness							
	Let go of judgments about others							
	Used problem-solving skills to strengthen relationships							
	Said no and established limits when necessary							
	Expressed a mindful interest in others							
SPIRITUAL	Used prayer or meditation to help myself							
	Sought or created meaning in my life							
	Allowed myself to be inspired or to inspire others							
	Honored my values and beliefs							
	Attended religious or spiritual services							

MONDAY

DATE / /

Skills practiced

MINDFULNESS	EMOTION REGULATION	DISTRESS TOLERANCE	INTERPERSONAL EFFECTIVENESS

Things that I'm thankful for

1.
2.
3.

Goals I worked towards

Today's shining moment

Notes and reminders

DAYS SOBER OR NUMBER OF DAYS SINCE ENGAGING IN A HARMFUL OR DESTRUCTIVE BEHAVIOR

BEHAVIOR	DAYS SINCE

TUESDAY

Skills practiced

MINDFULNESS	EMOTION REGULATION	DISTRESS TOLERANCE	INTERPERSONAL EFFECTIVENESS

Things that I'm thankful for

1.
2.
3.

Goals I worked towards

Today's **shining moment**

Notes and reminders

DAYS SOBER OR NUMBER OF DAYS SINCE ENGAGING IN A HARMFUL OR DESTRUCTIVE BEHAVIOR	BEHAVIOR	DAYS SINCE

WEDNESDAY

Skills practiced

MINDFULNESS	EMOTION REGULATION	DISTRESS TOLERANCE	INTERPERSONAL EFFECTIVENESS

Things that I'm thankful for

1.
2.
3.

Goals I worked towards

Today's **shining moment**

Notes and reminders

DAYS SOBER OR NUMBER OF DAYS SINCE ENGAGING IN A HARMFUL OR DESTRUCTIVE BEHAVIOR	BEHAVIOR	DAYS SINCE

THURSDAY

DATE   /   /

Skills practiced

MINDFULNESS	EMOTION REGULATION	DISTRESS TOLERANCE	INTERPERSONAL EFFECTIVENESS

Things that I'm **thankful** for

1.
2.
3.

Goals I worked towards

Today's **shining moment**

Notes and reminders

DAYS SOBER
OR NUMBER OF DAYS SINCE ENGAGING IN A HARMFUL OR DESTRUCTIVE BEHAVIOR

BEHAVIOR	DAYS SINCE

FRIDAY

DATE   /   /

Skills practiced

MINDFULNESS	EMOTION REGULATION	DISTRESS TOLERANCE	INTERPERSONAL EFFECTIVENESS

Things that I'm **thankful** for

1.
2.
3.

Goals I worked towards

Today's **shining moment**

Notes and reminders

DAYS SOBER
OR NUMBER OF DAYS SINCE ENGAGING IN A HARMFUL OR DESTRUCTIVE BEHAVIOR

BEHAVIOR	DAYS SINCE

SATURDAY

DATE / /

Skills practiced

MINDFULNESS	EMOTION REGULATION	DISTRESS TOLERANCE	INTERPERSONAL EFFECTIVENESS

Things that I'm thankful for

1.
2.
3.

Goals I worked towards

Today's shining moment

Notes and reminders

DAYS SOBER
OR NUMBER
OF DAYS SINCE
ENGAGING IN
A HARMFUL OR
DESTRUCTIVE
BEHAVIOR

BEHAVIOR	DAYS SINCE

SUNDAY

DATE / /

Skills practiced

MINDFULNESS	EMOTION REGULATION	DISTRESS TOLERANCE	INTERPERSONAL EFFECTIVENESS

Things that I'm thankful for

1.
2.
3.

Goals I worked towards

Today's shining moment

Notes and reminders

DAYS SOBER
OR NUMBER
OF DAYS SINCE
ENGAGING IN
A HARMFUL OR
DESTRUCTIVE
BEHAVIOR

BEHAVIOR	DAYS SINCE

SELF-CARE ASSESSMENT

Over the past 28 days, how often have you engaged in these specific self-care methods?

SCORING

4 **Always**

3 **Often**

2 **Sometimes**

1 **Rarely**

0 Not applicable to me at this time

PHYSICAL CARE	SCORE
Ate small balanced meals throughout the day	
Exercised for at least 15–20 minutes each day	
Followed preventive care instructions	
Bathed and brushed teeth daily	
Balanced sleep	
Refrained from self-medicating with alcohol, drugs, or prescription medicine	
Treated illness promptly	

TOTAL SCORE FOR THIS SECTION

EMOTIONAL CARE	SCORE
Attended all scheduled treatment and therapy appointments	
Made time for hobbies and enjoyable activities	
Politely said no to unwanted requests	
Let others know when I needed extra help	
Spent time with friends and loved ones	
Validated my own emotions, thoughts, and experiences	
Practiced self-compassion	

TOTAL SCORE FOR THIS SECTION

TOTAL SCORE PER SECTION

20-28	**Excellent!** You're doing a great job of taking care of yourself in this area.
11-19	**Very good.** Identify and address any gaps in self-care.
Below 10	**No one is perfect.** Is this an area of growth for you?

Remember, a score of zero (not applicable) in any area may lower your section score.

RELATIONAL CARE	SCORE
Stayed connected to friends and family members	
Set aside time to spend with people I care about	
Told people close to me that they were important	
Apologized or made repairs when I was wrong	
Expressed appreciation and thankfulness to others	
Empathized with others or thought about problems from their perspective	
Established limits and boundaries when necessary	

TOTAL SCORE FOR THIS SECTION

SPIRITUAL CARE	SCORE
Attended religious or spiritual services	
Spent time with others who share similar beliefs	
Sought spiritual direction or guidance	
Prayed or asked someone to pray for me	
Practiced mindfulness and/or meditation	
Identified important values and sought meaning in my life	
Read or watched things that helped to inspire me	

TOTAL SCORE FOR THIS SECTION

THE WEEK AHEAD

Daily self-care tracker

		M	T	W	T	F	S	S
PHYSICAL	Exercised for at least 10–15 minutes	✓/✗						
	Took prescribed medications as directed							
	Refrained from self-medicating							
	Got enough sleep							
	Ate balanced meals							
EMOTIONAL	Skillfully tolerated distressing moments							
	Validated my own thoughts, emotions, and experiences							
	Practiced self-compassion							
	Engaged in mindful breathing or breath counting							
	Observed and described feelings mindfully							
RELATIONAL	Practiced empathy and unconditional kindness							
	Let go of judgments about others							
	Used problem-solving skills to strengthen relationships							
	Said no and established limits when necessary							
	Expressed a mindful interest in others							
SPIRITUAL	Used prayer or meditation to help myself							
	Sought or created meaning in my life							
	Allowed myself to be inspired or to inspire others							
	Honored my values and beliefs							
	Attended religious or spiritual services							

MONDAY

DATE / /

Skills practiced

MINDFULNESS	EMOTION REGULATION	DISTRESS TOLERANCE	INTERPERSONAL EFFECTIVENESS

Things that I'm **thankful** for

1.

2.

3.

Goals I worked towards

Today's **shining moment**

Notes and reminders

DAYS SOBER
OR NUMBER OF DAYS SINCE ENGAGING IN A HARMFUL OR DESTRUCTIVE BEHAVIOR

BEHAVIOR	DAYS SINCE

TUESDAY

Skills practiced

MINDFULNESS	EMOTION REGULATION	DISTRESS TOLERANCE	INTERPERSONAL EFFECTIVENESS

Things that I'm **thankful** for

1.
2.
3.

Goals I worked towards

Today's **shining moment**

Notes and reminders

DAYS SOBER
OR NUMBER OF DAYS SINCE ENGAGING IN A HARMFUL OR DESTRUCTIVE BEHAVIOR

BEHAVIOR

DAYS SINCE

WEDNESDAY

DATE / /

Skills practiced

MINDFULNESS	EMOTION REGULATION	DISTRESS TOLERANCE	INTERPERSONAL EFFECTIVENESS

Things that I'm **thankful** for

1.
2.
3.

Goals I worked towards

Today's **shining moment**

Notes and reminders

DAYS SOBER
OR NUMBER OF DAYS SINCE ENGAGING IN A HARMFUL OR DESTRUCTIVE BEHAVIOR

BEHAVIOR

DAYS SINCE

THURSDAY

DATE   /   /

Skills practiced

MINDFULNESS	EMOTION REGULATION	DISTRESS TOLERANCE	INTERPERSONAL EFFECTIVENESS

Things that I'm **thankful** for   **Goals** I worked towards   Today's **shining moment**

1.

2.

3.

Notes and reminders

DAYS SOBER
OR NUMBER OF DAYS SINCE ENGAGING IN A HARMFUL OR DESTRUCTIVE BEHAVIOR

BEHAVIOR	DAYS SINCE

FRIDAY

DATE   /   /

Skills practiced

MINDFULNESS	EMOTION REGULATION	DISTRESS TOLERANCE	INTERPERSONAL EFFECTIVENESS

Things that I'm **thankful** for   **Goals** I worked towards   Today's **shining moment**

1.

2.

3.

Notes and reminders

DAYS SOBER
OR NUMBER OF DAYS SINCE ENGAGING IN A HARMFUL OR DESTRUCTIVE BEHAVIOR

BEHAVIOR	DAYS SINCE

SATURDAY

DATE / /

Skills practiced

MINDFULNESS	EMOTION REGULATION	DISTRESS TOLERANCE	INTERPERSONAL EFFECTIVENESS

Things that I'm **thankful** for

1.
2.
3.

Goals I worked towards

Today's **shining moment**

Notes and reminders

DAYS SOBER OR NUMBER OF DAYS SINCE ENGAGING IN A HARMFUL OR DESTRUCTIVE BEHAVIOR	BEHAVIOR	DAYS SINCE

SUNDAY

DATE / /

Skills practiced

MINDFULNESS	EMOTION REGULATION	DISTRESS TOLERANCE	INTERPERSONAL EFFECTIVENESS

Things that I'm **thankful** for

1.
2.
3.

Goals I worked towards

Today's **shining moment**

Notes and reminders

DAYS SOBER OR NUMBER OF DAYS SINCE ENGAGING IN A HARMFUL OR DESTRUCTIVE BEHAVIOR	BEHAVIOR	DAYS SINCE

THE WEEK AHEAD

Daily self-care tracker

		M	T	W	T	F	S	S
PHYSICAL	Exercised for at least 10–15 minutes	✓	✗					
	Took prescribed medications as directed							
	Refrained from self-medicating							
	Got enough sleep							
	Ate balanced meals							
EMOTIONAL	Skillfully tolerated distressing moments							
	Validated my own thoughts, emotions, and experiences							
	Practiced self-compassion							
	Engaged in mindful breathing or breath counting							
	Observed and described feelings mindfully							
RELATIONAL	Practiced empathy and unconditional kindness							
	Let go of judgments about others							
	Used problem-solving skills to strengthen relationships							
	Said no and established limits when necessary							
	Expressed a mindful interest in others							
SPIRITUAL	Used prayer or meditation to help myself							
	Sought or created meaning in my life							
	Allowed myself to be inspired or to inspire others							
	Honored my values and beliefs							
	Attended religious or spiritual services							

MONDAY

DATE   /   /

Skills practiced

MINDFULNESS	EMOTION REGULATION	DISTRESS TOLERANCE	INTERPERSONAL EFFECTIVENESS

Things that I'm **thankful** for

1.
2.
3.

Goals I worked towards

Today's **shining moment**

Notes and reminders

DAYS SOBER
OR NUMBER OF DAYS SINCE ENGAGING IN A HARMFUL OR DESTRUCTIVE BEHAVIOR

BEHAVIOR	DAYS SINCE

TUESDAY

Skills practiced

MINDFULNESS	EMOTION REGULATION	DISTRESS TOLERANCE	INTERPERSONAL EFFECTIVENESS

Things that I'm **thankful** for

1.
2.
3.

Goals I worked towards

Today's **shining moment**

Notes and reminders

DAYS SOBER
OR NUMBER OF DAYS SINCE ENGAGING IN A HARMFUL OR DESTRUCTIVE BEHAVIOR

BEHAVIOR	DAYS SINCE

WEDNESDAY

DATE / /

Skills practiced

MINDFULNESS	EMOTION REGULATION	DISTRESS TOLERANCE	INTERPERSONAL EFFECTIVENESS

Things that I'm **thankful** for

1.
2.
3.

Goals I worked towards

Today's **shining moment**

Notes and reminders

DAYS SOBER
OR NUMBER OF DAYS SINCE ENGAGING IN A HARMFUL OR DESTRUCTIVE BEHAVIOR

BEHAVIOR	DAYS SINCE

THURSDAY

Skills practiced

MINDFULNESS	EMOTION REGULATION	DISTRESS TOLERANCE	INTERPERSONAL EFFECTIVENESS

Things that I'm **thankful** for

1.
2.
3.

Goals I worked towards

Today's **shining moment**

Notes and reminders

DAYS SOBER
OR NUMBER OF DAYS SINCE ENGAGING IN A HARMFUL OR DESTRUCTIVE BEHAVIOR

BEHAVIOR	DAYS SINCE

FRIDAY

DATE / /

Skills practiced

MINDFULNESS	EMOTION REGULATION	DISTRESS TOLERANCE	INTERPERSONAL EFFECTIVENESS

Things that I'm **thankful** for

1.
2.
3.

Goals I worked towards

Today's **shining moment**

Notes and reminders

DAYS SOBER
OR NUMBER OF DAYS SINCE ENGAGING IN A HARMFUL OR DESTRUCTIVE BEHAVIOR

BEHAVIOR	DAYS SINCE

SATURDAY

Skills practiced

MINDFULNESS	EMOTION REGULATION	DISTRESS TOLERANCE	INTERPERSONAL EFFECTIVENESS

Things that I'm **thankful** for

1.
2.
3.

Goals I worked towards

Today's **shining moment**

Notes and reminders

DAYS SOBER OR NUMBER OF DAYS SINCE ENGAGING IN A HARMFUL OR DESTRUCTIVE BEHAVIOR

BEHAVIOR	DAYS SINCE

SUNDAY

DATE / /

Skills practiced

MINDFULNESS	EMOTION REGULATION	DISTRESS TOLERANCE	INTERPERSONAL EFFECTIVENESS

Things that I'm **thankful** for

1.
2.
3.

Goals I worked towards

Today's **shining moment**

Notes and reminders

DAYS SOBER OR NUMBER OF DAYS SINCE ENGAGING IN A HARMFUL OR DESTRUCTIVE BEHAVIOR

BEHAVIOR	DAYS SINCE

THE WEEK AHEAD

Daily self-care tracker

		M	T	W	T	F	S	S
PHYSICAL	Exercised for at least 10–15 minutes	✓	✗					
	Took prescribed medications as directed							
	Refrained from self-medicating							
	Got enough sleep							
	Ate balanced meals							
EMOTIONAL	Skillfully tolerated distressing moments							
	Validated my own thoughts, emotions, and experiences							
	Practiced self-compassion							
	Engaged in mindful breathing or breath counting							
	Observed and described feelings mindfully							
RELATIONAL	Practiced empathy and unconditional kindness							
	Let go of judgments about others							
	Used problem-solving skills to strengthen relationships							
	Said no and established limits when necessary							
	Expressed a mindful interest in others							
SPIRITUAL	Used prayer or meditation to help myself							
	Sought or created meaning in my life							
	Allowed myself to be inspired or to inspire others							
	Honored my values and beliefs							
	Attended religious or spiritual services							

MONDAY

DATE / /

Skills practiced

MINDFULNESS	EMOTION REGULATION	DISTRESS TOLERANCE	INTERPERSONAL EFFECTIVENESS

Things that I'm **thankful** for

1.
2.
3.

Goals I worked towards

Today's **shining moment**

Notes and reminders

DAYS SOBER
OR NUMBER OF DAYS SINCE ENGAGING IN A HARMFUL OR DESTRUCTIVE BEHAVIOR

BEHAVIOR	DAYS SINCE

TUESDAY

Skills practiced

MINDFULNESS	EMOTION REGULATION	DISTRESS TOLERANCE	INTERPERSONAL EFFECTIVENESS

Things that I'm **thankful** for

1.
2.
3.

Goals I worked towards

Today's **shining moment**

Notes and reminders

DAYS SOBER
OR NUMBER OF DAYS SINCE ENGAGING IN A HARMFUL OR DESTRUCTIVE BEHAVIOR

BEHAVIOR	DAYS SINCE

WEDNESDAY

Skills practiced

MINDFULNESS	EMOTION REGULATION	DISTRESS TOLERANCE	INTERPERSONAL EFFECTIVENESS

Things that I'm **thankful** for

1.
2.
3.

Goals I worked towards

Today's **shining moment**

Notes and reminders

DAYS SOBER
OR NUMBER OF DAYS SINCE ENGAGING IN A HARMFUL OR DESTRUCTIVE BEHAVIOR

BEHAVIOR	DAYS SINCE

THURSDAY

Skills practiced

MINDFULNESS	EMOTION REGULATION	DISTRESS TOLERANCE	INTERPERSONAL EFFECTIVENESS

Things that I'm **thankful** for

1.
2.
3.

Goals I worked towards

Today's **shining moment**

Notes and reminders

DAYS SOBER OR NUMBER OF DAYS SINCE ENGAGING IN A HARMFUL OR DESTRUCTIVE BEHAVIOR

BEHAVIOR	DAYS SINCE

FRIDAY

Skills practiced

MINDFULNESS	EMOTION REGULATION	DISTRESS TOLERANCE	INTERPERSONAL EFFECTIVENESS

Things that I'm **thankful** for

1.
2.
3.

Goals I worked towards

Today's **shining moment**

Notes and reminders

DAYS SOBER OR NUMBER OF DAYS SINCE ENGAGING IN A HARMFUL OR DESTRUCTIVE BEHAVIOR

BEHAVIOR	DAYS SINCE

SATURDAY

DATE   /   /

Skills practiced

MINDFULNESS	EMOTION REGULATION	DISTRESS TOLERANCE	INTERPERSONAL EFFECTIVENESS

Things that I'm **thankful** for

1.
2.
3.

Goals I worked towards

Today's **shining moment**

Notes and reminders

DAYS SOBER
OR NUMBER OF DAYS SINCE ENGAGING IN A HARMFUL OR DESTRUCTIVE BEHAVIOR

BEHAVIOR	DAYS SINCE
	☐ ☐ ☐
	☐ ☐ ☐
	☐ ☐ ☐

SUNDAY

DATE   /   /

Skills practiced

MINDFULNESS	EMOTION REGULATION	DISTRESS TOLERANCE	INTERPERSONAL EFFECTIVENESS

Things that I'm **thankful** for

1.
2.
3.

Goals I worked towards

Today's **shining moment**

Notes and reminders

DAYS SOBER
OR NUMBER OF DAYS SINCE ENGAGING IN A HARMFUL OR DESTRUCTIVE BEHAVIOR

BEHAVIOR	DAYS SINCE
	☐ ☐ ☐
	☐ ☐ ☐
	☐ ☐ ☐

THE WEEK AHEAD

Daily self-care tracker

		M	T	W	T	F	S	S
PHYSICAL	Exercised for at least 10–15 minutes	✓/✗						
	Took prescribed medications as directed							
	Refrained from self-medicating							
	Got enough sleep							
	Ate balanced meals							
EMOTIONAL	Skillfully tolerated distressing moments							
	Validated my own thoughts, emotions, and experiences							
	Practiced self-compassion							
	Engaged in mindful breathing or breath counting							
	Observed and described feelings mindfully							
RELATIONAL	Practiced empathy and unconditional kindness							
	Let go of judgments about others							
	Used problem-solving skills to strengthen relationships							
	Said no and established limits when necessary							
	Expressed a mindful interest in others							
SPIRITUAL	Used prayer or meditation to help myself							
	Sought or created meaning in my life							
	Allowed myself to be inspired or to inspire others							
	Honored my values and beliefs							
	Attended religious or spiritual services							

MONDAY

DATE /   /

Skills practiced

MINDFULNESS	EMOTION REGULATION	DISTRESS TOLERANCE	INTERPERSONAL EFFECTIVENESS

Things that I'm thankful for

1.
2.
3.

Goals I worked towards

Today's shining moment

Notes and reminders

DAYS SOBER
OR NUMBER OF DAYS SINCE ENGAGING IN A HARMFUL OR DESTRUCTIVE BEHAVIOR

BEHAVIOR	DAYS SINCE

TUESDAY

DATE   /   /

Skills practiced

MINDFULNESS	EMOTION REGULATION	DISTRESS TOLERANCE	INTERPERSONAL EFFECTIVENESS

Things that I'm **thankful** for

1.
2.
3.

Goals I worked towards

Today's **shining moment**

Notes and reminders

DAYS SOBER OR NUMBER OF DAYS SINCE ENGAGING IN A HARMFUL OR DESTRUCTIVE BEHAVIOR	BEHAVIOR	DAYS SINCE

WEDNESDAY

DATE   /   /

Skills practiced

MINDFULNESS	EMOTION REGULATION	DISTRESS TOLERANCE	INTERPERSONAL EFFECTIVENESS

Things that I'm **thankful** for

1.
2.
3.

Goals I worked towards

Today's **shining moment**

Notes and reminders

DAYS SOBER OR NUMBER OF DAYS SINCE ENGAGING IN A HARMFUL OR DESTRUCTIVE BEHAVIOR	BEHAVIOR	DAYS SINCE

THURSDAY

Skills practiced

MINDFULNESS	EMOTION REGULATION	DISTRESS TOLERANCE	INTERPERSONAL EFFECTIVENESS

Things that I'm **thankful** for

1.
2.
3.

Goals I worked towards

Today's **shining moment**

Notes and reminders

DAYS SOBER
OR NUMBER OF DAYS SINCE ENGAGING IN A HARMFUL OR DESTRUCTIVE BEHAVIOR

BEHAVIOR	DAYS SINCE

FRIDAY

Skills practiced

MINDFULNESS	EMOTION REGULATION	DISTRESS TOLERANCE	INTERPERSONAL EFFECTIVENESS

Things that I'm **thankful** for

1.
2.
3.

Goals I worked towards

Today's **shining moment**

Notes and reminders

DAYS SOBER
OR NUMBER OF DAYS SINCE ENGAGING IN A HARMFUL OR DESTRUCTIVE BEHAVIOR

BEHAVIOR	DAYS SINCE

SATURDAY

DATE / /

Skills practiced

MINDFULNESS	EMOTION REGULATION	DISTRESS TOLERANCE	INTERPERSONAL EFFECTIVENESS

Things that I'm **thankful** for

1.
2.
3.

Goals I worked towards

Today's **shining moment**

Notes and reminders

DAYS SOBER
OR NUMBER OF DAYS SINCE ENGAGING IN A HARMFUL OR DESTRUCTIVE BEHAVIOR

BEHAVIOR

DAYS SINCE

SUNDAY

DATE / /

Skills practiced

MINDFULNESS	EMOTION REGULATION	DISTRESS TOLERANCE	INTERPERSONAL EFFECTIVENESS

Things that I'm **thankful** for

1.
2.
3.

Goals I worked towards

Today's **shining moment**

Notes and reminders

DAYS SOBER
OR NUMBER OF DAYS SINCE ENGAGING IN A HARMFUL OR DESTRUCTIVE BEHAVIOR

BEHAVIOR

DAYS SINCE

SELF-CARE ASSESSMENT

Over the past 28 days, how often have you engaged in these specific self-care methods?

PHYSICAL CARE	SCORE
Ate small balanced meals throughout the day	
Exercised for at least 15–20 minutes each day	
Followed preventive care instructions	
Bathed and brushed teeth daily	
Balanced sleep	
Refrained from self-medicating with alcohol, drugs, or prescription medicine	
Treated illness promptly	

TOTAL SCORE FOR THIS SECTION

EMOTIONAL CARE	SCORE
Attended all scheduled treatment and therapy appointments	
Made time for hobbies and enjoyable activities	
Politely said no to unwanted requests	
Let others know when I needed extra help	
Spent time with friends and loved ones	
Validated my own emotions, thoughts, and experiences	
Practiced self-compassion	

TOTAL SCORE FOR THIS SECTION

TOTAL SCORE PER SECTION

20-28	**Excellent!** You're doing a great job of taking care of yourself in this area.
11-19	**Very good.** Identify and address any gaps in self-care.
Below 10	**No one is perfect.** Is this an area of growth for you?

Remember, a score of zero (not applicable) in any area may lower your section score.

RELATIONAL CARE	SCORE
Stayed connected to friends and family members	
Set aside time to spend with people I care about	
Told people close to me that they were important	
Apologized or made repairs when I was wrong	
Expressed appreciation and thankfulness to others	
Empathized with others or thought about problems from their perspective	
Established limits and boundaries when necessary	

TOTAL SCORE FOR THIS SECTION

SPIRITUAL CARE	SCORE
Attended religious or spiritual services	
Spent time with others who share similar beliefs	
Sought spiritual direction or guidance	
Prayed or asked someone to pray for me	
Practiced mindfulness and/or meditation	
Identified important values and sought meaning in my life	
Read or watched things that helped to inspire me	

TOTAL SCORE FOR THIS SECTION

THE WEEK AHEAD

Daily self-care tracker

		M	T	W	T	F	S	S
PHYSICAL	Exercised for at least 10–15 minutes	✓						
	Took prescribed medications as directed	✗						
	Refrained from self-medicating							
	Got enough sleep							
	Ate balanced meals							
EMOTIONAL	Skillfully tolerated distressing moments							
	Validated my own thoughts, emotions, and experiences							
	Practiced self-compassion							
	Engaged in mindful breathing or breath counting							
	Observed and described feelings mindfully							
RELATIONAL	Practiced empathy and unconditional kindness							
	Let go of judgments about others							
	Used problem-solving skills to strengthen relationships							
	Said no and established limits when necessary							
	Expressed a mindful interest in others							
SPIRITUAL	Used prayer or meditation to help myself							
	Sought or created meaning in my life							
	Allowed myself to be inspired or to inspire others							
	Honored my values and beliefs							
	Attended religious or spiritual services							

MONDAY

DATE ___ / ___ / ___

Skills practiced

MINDFULNESS	EMOTION REGULATION	DISTRESS TOLERANCE	INTERPERSONAL EFFECTIVENESS

Things that I'm **thankful** for

1. _____
2. _____
3. _____

Goals I worked towards

_____
_____
_____

Today's **shining moment**

_____
_____
_____

Notes and reminders

_____
_____
_____

DAYS SOBER OR NUMBER OF DAYS SINCE ENGAGING IN A HARMFUL OR DESTRUCTIVE BEHAVIOR	BEHAVIOR	DAYS SINCE
	_____	▢▢
	_____	▢▢
	_____	▢▢

TUESDAY

DATE ___/___/___

Skills practiced

MINDFULNESS	EMOTION REGULATION	DISTRESS TOLERANCE	INTERPERSONAL EFFECTIVENESS

Things that I'm **thankful** for

1.
2.
3.

Goals I worked towards

Today's **shining moment**

Notes and reminders

DAYS SOBER
OR NUMBER OF DAYS SINCE ENGAGING IN A HARMFUL OR DESTRUCTIVE BEHAVIOR

BEHAVIOR	DAYS SINCE

WEDNESDAY

DATE ___/___/___

Skills practiced

MINDFULNESS	EMOTION REGULATION	DISTRESS TOLERANCE	INTERPERSONAL EFFECTIVENESS

Things that I'm **thankful** for

1.
2.
3.

Goals I worked towards

Today's **shining moment**

Notes and reminders

DAYS SOBER
OR NUMBER OF DAYS SINCE ENGAGING IN A HARMFUL OR DESTRUCTIVE BEHAVIOR

BEHAVIOR	DAYS SINCE

THURSDAY

DATE / /

Skills practiced

MINDFULNESS	EMOTION REGULATION	DISTRESS TOLERANCE	INTERPERSONAL EFFECTIVENESS

Things that I'm **thankful** for

1.
2.
3.

Goals I worked towards

Today's **shining moment**

Notes and reminders

DAYS SOBER
OR NUMBER OF DAYS SINCE ENGAGING IN A HARMFUL OR DESTRUCTIVE BEHAVIOR

BEHAVIOR	DAYS SINCE

FRIDAY

DATE / /

Skills practiced

MINDFULNESS	EMOTION REGULATION	DISTRESS TOLERANCE	INTERPERSONAL EFFECTIVENESS

Things that I'm **thankful** for

1.
2.
3.

Goals I worked towards

Today's **shining moment**

Notes and reminders

DAYS SOBER
OR NUMBER OF DAYS SINCE ENGAGING IN A HARMFUL OR DESTRUCTIVE BEHAVIOR

BEHAVIOR	DAYS SINCE

SATURDAY

DATE   /   /

Skills practiced

MINDFULNESS	EMOTION REGULATION	DISTRESS TOLERANCE	INTERPERSONAL EFFECTIVENESS

Things that I'm thankful for

1.
2.
3.

Goals I worked towards

Today's shining moment

Notes and reminders

DAYS SOBER OR NUMBER OF DAYS SINCE ENGAGING IN A HARMFUL OR DESTRUCTIVE BEHAVIOR	BEHAVIOR	DAYS SINCE
		▢▢▢
		▢▢▢
		▢▢▢

SUNDAY

DATE   /   /

Skills practiced

MINDFULNESS	EMOTION REGULATION	DISTRESS TOLERANCE	INTERPERSONAL EFFECTIVENESS

Things that I'm thankful for

1.
2.
3.

Goals I worked towards

Today's shining moment

Notes and reminders

DAYS SOBER OR NUMBER OF DAYS SINCE ENGAGING IN A HARMFUL OR DESTRUCTIVE BEHAVIOR	BEHAVIOR	DAYS SINCE
		▢▢▢
		▢▢▢
		▢▢▢

THE WEEK AHEAD

Daily self-care tracker

		M	T	W	T	F	S	S
PHYSICAL	Exercised for at least 10–15 minutes	✓						
	Took prescribed medications as directed	✗						
	Refrained from self-medicating							
	Got enough sleep							
	Ate balanced meals							
EMOTIONAL	Skillfully tolerated distressing moments							
	Validated my own thoughts, emotions, and experiences							
	Practiced self-compassion							
	Engaged in mindful breathing or breath counting							
	Observed and described feelings mindfully							
RELATIONAL	Practiced empathy and unconditional kindness							
	Let go of judgments about others							
	Used problem-solving skills to strengthen relationships							
	Said no and established limits when necessary							
	Expressed a mindful interest in others							
SPIRITUAL	Used prayer or meditation to help myself							
	Sought or created meaning in my life							
	Allowed myself to be inspired or to inspire others							
	Honored my values and beliefs							
	Attended religious or spiritual services							

MONDAY

DATE / /

Skills practiced

MINDFULNESS	EMOTION REGULATION	DISTRESS TOLERANCE	INTERPERSONAL EFFECTIVENESS

Things that I'm **thankful** for

1.
2.
3.

Goals I worked towards

Today's **shining moment**

Notes and reminders

DAYS SOBER
OR NUMBER OF DAYS SINCE ENGAGING IN A HARMFUL OR DESTRUCTIVE BEHAVIOR

BEHAVIOR	DAYS SINCE

TUESDAY

Skills practiced

MINDFULNESS	EMOTION REGULATION	DISTRESS TOLERANCE	INTERPERSONAL EFFECTIVENESS

Things that I'm **thankful** for

1.
2.
3.

Goals I worked towards

Today's **shining moment**

Notes and reminders

DAYS SOBER
OR NUMBER OF DAYS SINCE ENGAGING IN A HARMFUL OR DESTRUCTIVE BEHAVIOR

BEHAVIOR	DAYS SINCE

WEDNESDAY

DATE / /

Skills practiced

MINDFULNESS	EMOTION REGULATION	DISTRESS TOLERANCE	INTERPERSONAL EFFECTIVENESS

Things that I'm **thankful** for

1.
2.
3.

Goals I worked towards

Today's **shining moment**

Notes and reminders

DAYS SOBER
OR NUMBER OF DAYS SINCE ENGAGING IN A HARMFUL OR DESTRUCTIVE BEHAVIOR

BEHAVIOR	DAYS SINCE

THURSDAY

Skills practiced

MINDFULNESS	EMOTION REGULATION	DISTRESS TOLERANCE	INTERPERSONAL EFFECTIVENESS

Things that I'm **thankful** for

1.
2.
3.

Goals I worked towards

Today's **shining moment**

Notes and reminders

DAYS SOBER
OR NUMBER OF DAYS SINCE ENGAGING IN A HARMFUL OR DESTRUCTIVE BEHAVIOR

BEHAVIOR	DAYS SINCE

FRIDAY

Skills practiced

MINDFULNESS	EMOTION REGULATION	DISTRESS TOLERANCE	INTERPERSONAL EFFECTIVENESS

Things that I'm **thankful** for

1.
2.
3.

Goals I worked towards

Today's **shining moment**

Notes and reminders

DAYS SOBER
OR NUMBER OF DAYS SINCE ENGAGING IN A HARMFUL OR DESTRUCTIVE BEHAVIOR

BEHAVIOR	DAYS SINCE

SATURDAY

DATE / /

Skills practiced

MINDFULNESS	EMOTION REGULATION	DISTRESS TOLERANCE	INTERPERSONAL EFFECTIVENESS

Things that I'm **thankful** for

1.
2.
3.

Goals I worked towards

Today's **shining moment**

Notes and reminders

DAYS SOBER OR NUMBER OF DAYS SINCE ENGAGING IN A HARMFUL OR DESTRUCTIVE BEHAVIOR

BEHAVIOR	DAYS SINCE

SUNDAY

DATE / /

Skills practiced

MINDFULNESS	EMOTION REGULATION	DISTRESS TOLERANCE	INTERPERSONAL EFFECTIVENESS

Things that I'm **thankful** for

1.
2.
3.

Goals I worked towards

Today's **shining moment**

Notes and reminders

DAYS SOBER OR NUMBER OF DAYS SINCE ENGAGING IN A HARMFUL OR DESTRUCTIVE BEHAVIOR

BEHAVIOR	DAYS SINCE

THE WEEK AHEAD

Daily self-care tracker

		M	T	W	T	F	S	S
PHYSICAL	Exercised for at least 10-15 minutes	✓✗						
	Took prescribed medications as directed							
	Refrained from self-medicating							
	Got enough sleep							
	Ate balanced meals							
EMOTIONAL	Skillfully tolerated distressing moments							
	Validated my own thoughts, emotions, and experiences							
	Practiced self-compassion							
	Engaged in mindful breathing or breath counting							
	Observed and described feelings mindfully							
RELATIONAL	Practiced empathy and unconditional kindness							
	Let go of judgments about others							
	Used problem-solving skills to strengthen relationships							
	Said no and established limits when necessary							
	Expressed a mindful interest in others							
SPIRITUAL	Used prayer or meditation to help myself							
	Sought or created meaning in my life							
	Allowed myself to be inspired or to inspire others							
	Honored my values and beliefs							
	Attended religious or spiritual services							

MONDAY

DATE   /   /

Skills practiced

MINDFULNESS	EMOTION REGULATION	DISTRESS TOLERANCE	INTERPERSONAL EFFECTIVENESS

Things that I'm **thankful** for

1.
2.
3.

Goals I worked towards

Today's **shining moment**

Notes and reminders

DAYS SOBER OR NUMBER OF DAYS SINCE ENGAGING IN A HARMFUL OR DESTRUCTIVE BEHAVIOR

BEHAVIOR	DAYS SINCE

TUESDAY

Skills practiced

MINDFULNESS	EMOTION REGULATION	DISTRESS TOLERANCE	INTERPERSONAL EFFECTIVENESS

Things that I'm **thankful** for

1.
2.
3.

Goals I worked towards

Today's **shining moment**

Notes and reminders

DAYS SOBER
OR NUMBER OF DAYS SINCE ENGAGING IN A HARMFUL OR DESTRUCTIVE BEHAVIOR

BEHAVIOR	DAYS SINCE

WEDNESDAY

DATE / /

Skills practiced

MINDFULNESS	EMOTION REGULATION	DISTRESS TOLERANCE	INTERPERSONAL EFFECTIVENESS

Things that I'm **thankful** for

1.
2.
3.

Goals I worked towards

Today's **shining moment**

Notes and reminders

DAYS SOBER
OR NUMBER OF DAYS SINCE ENGAGING IN A HARMFUL OR DESTRUCTIVE BEHAVIOR

BEHAVIOR	DAYS SINCE

THURSDAY

Skills practiced

MINDFULNESS	EMOTION REGULATION	DISTRESS TOLERANCE	INTERPERSONAL EFFECTIVENESS

Things that I'm **thankful** for

1.
2.
3.

Goals I worked towards

Today's **shining moment**

Notes and reminders

DAYS SOBER OR NUMBER OF DAYS SINCE ENGAGING IN A HARMFUL OR DESTRUCTIVE BEHAVIOR	BEHAVIOR	DAYS SINCE

FRIDAY

Skills practiced

MINDFULNESS	EMOTION REGULATION	DISTRESS TOLERANCE	INTERPERSONAL EFFECTIVENESS

Things that I'm **thankful** for

1.
2.
3.

Goals I worked towards

Today's **shining moment**

Notes and reminders

DAYS SOBER OR NUMBER OF DAYS SINCE ENGAGING IN A HARMFUL OR DESTRUCTIVE BEHAVIOR	BEHAVIOR	DAYS SINCE

SATURDAY

DATE / /

Skills practiced

MINDFULNESS	EMOTION REGULATION	DISTRESS TOLERANCE	INTERPERSONAL EFFECTIVENESS

Things that I'm **thankful** for

1.
2.
3.

Goals I worked towards

Today's **shining moment**

Notes and reminders

DAYS SOBER
OR NUMBER OF DAYS SINCE ENGAGING IN A HARMFUL OR DESTRUCTIVE BEHAVIOR

BEHAVIOR	DAYS SINCE

SUNDAY

DATE / /

Skills practiced

MINDFULNESS	EMOTION REGULATION	DISTRESS TOLERANCE	INTERPERSONAL EFFECTIVENESS

Things that I'm **thankful** for

1.
2.
3.

Goals I worked towards

Today's **shining moment**

Notes and reminders

DAYS SOBER
OR NUMBER OF DAYS SINCE ENGAGING IN A HARMFUL OR DESTRUCTIVE BEHAVIOR

BEHAVIOR	DAYS SINCE

THE WEEK AHEAD

Daily self-care tracker

		M	T	W	T	F	S	S
PHYSICAL	Exercised for at least 10-15 minutes	✓/✗						
	Took prescribed medications as directed							
	Refrained from self-medicating							
	Got enough sleep							
	Ate balanced meals							
EMOTIONAL	Skillfully tolerated distressing moments							
	Validated my own thoughts, emotions, and experiences							
	Practiced self-compassion							
	Engaged in mindful breathing or breath counting							
	Observed and described feelings mindfully							
RELATIONAL	Practiced empathy and unconditional kindness							
	Let go of judgments about others							
	Used problem-solving skills to strengthen relationships							
	Said no and established limits when necessary							
	Expressed a mindful interest in others							
SPIRITUAL	Used prayer or meditation to help myself							
	Sought or created meaning in my life							
	Allowed myself to be inspired or to inspire others							
	Honored my values and beliefs							
	Attended religious or spiritual services							

MONDAY

DATE / /

Skills practiced

MINDFULNESS	EMOTION REGULATION	DISTRESS TOLERANCE	INTERPERSONAL EFFECTIVENESS

Things that I'm **thankful** for

1.

2.

3.

Goals I worked towards

Today's **shining moment**

Notes and reminders

DAYS SOBER OR NUMBER OF DAYS SINCE ENGAGING IN A HARMFUL OR DESTRUCTIVE BEHAVIOR

BEHAVIOR	DAYS SINCE

TUESDAY

DATE / /

Skills practiced

MINDFULNESS	EMOTION REGULATION	DISTRESS TOLERANCE	INTERPERSONAL EFFECTIVENESS

Things that I'm **thankful** for

1.
2.
3.

Goals I worked towards

Today's **shining moment**

Notes and reminders

DAYS SOBER OR NUMBER OF DAYS SINCE ENGAGING IN A HARMFUL OR DESTRUCTIVE BEHAVIOR

BEHAVIOR	DAYS SINCE

WEDNESDAY

DATE / /

Skills practiced

MINDFULNESS	EMOTION REGULATION	DISTRESS TOLERANCE	INTERPERSONAL EFFECTIVENESS

Things that I'm **thankful** for

1.
2.
3.

Goals I worked towards

Today's **shining moment**

Notes and reminders

DAYS SOBER OR NUMBER OF DAYS SINCE ENGAGING IN A HARMFUL OR DESTRUCTIVE BEHAVIOR

BEHAVIOR	DAYS SINCE

THURSDAY

Skills practiced

MINDFULNESS	EMOTION REGULATION	DISTRESS TOLERANCE	INTERPERSONAL EFFECTIVENESS

Things that I'm **thankful** for

1.

2.

3.

Goals I worked towards

Today's **shining moment**

Notes and reminders

DAYS SOBER
OR NUMBER OF DAYS SINCE ENGAGING IN A HARMFUL OR DESTRUCTIVE BEHAVIOR

BEHAVIOR	DAYS SINCE

FRIDAY

Skills practiced

MINDFULNESS	EMOTION REGULATION	DISTRESS TOLERANCE	INTERPERSONAL EFFECTIVENESS

Things that I'm **thankful** for

1.

2.

3.

Goals I worked towards

Today's **shining moment**

Notes and reminders

DAYS SOBER
OR NUMBER OF DAYS SINCE ENGAGING IN A HARMFUL OR DESTRUCTIVE BEHAVIOR

BEHAVIOR	DAYS SINCE

SATURDAY

DATE   /   /

Skills practiced

MINDFULNESS	EMOTION REGULATION	DISTRESS TOLERANCE	INTERPERSONAL EFFECTIVENESS

Things that I'm **thankful** for

1.
2.
3.

Goals I worked towards

Today's **shining moment**

Notes and reminders

DAYS SOBER
OR NUMBER OF DAYS SINCE ENGAGING IN A HARMFUL OR DESTRUCTIVE BEHAVIOR

BEHAVIOR	DAYS SINCE

SUNDAY

DATE   /   /

Skills practiced

MINDFULNESS	EMOTION REGULATION	DISTRESS TOLERANCE	INTERPERSONAL EFFECTIVENESS

Things that I'm **thankful** for

1.
2.
3.

Goals I worked towards

Today's **shining moment**

Notes and reminders

DAYS SOBER
OR NUMBER OF DAYS SINCE ENGAGING IN A HARMFUL OR DESTRUCTIVE BEHAVIOR

BEHAVIOR	DAYS SINCE

SELF-CARE ASSESSMENT

Over the past 28 days, how often have you engaged in these specific self-care methods?

SCORING

4	**Always**
3	**Often**
2	**Sometimes**
1	**Rarely**
0	Not applicable to me at this time

PHYSICAL CARE	SCORE
Ate small balanced meals throughout the day	
Exercised for at least 15–20 minutes each day	
Followed preventive care instructions	
Bathed and brushed teeth daily	
Balanced sleep	
Refrained from self-medicating with alcohol, drugs, or prescription medicine	
Treated illness promptly	

TOTAL SCORE FOR THIS SECTION

EMOTIONAL CARE	SCORE
Attended all scheduled treatment and therapy appointments	
Made time for hobbies and enjoyable activities	
Politely said no to unwanted requests	
Let others know when I needed extra help	
Spent time with friends and loved ones	
Validated my own emotions, thoughts, and experiences	
Practiced self-compassion	

TOTAL SCORE FOR THIS SECTION

TOTAL SCORE PER SECTION

20-28	**Excellent!** You're doing a great job of taking care of yourself in this area.
11-19	**Very good.** Identify and address any gaps in self-care.
Below 10	**No one is perfect.** Is this an area of growth for you?

Remember, a score of zero (not applicable) in any area may lower your section score.

RELATIONAL CARE	SCORE
Stayed connected to friends and family members	
Set aside time to spend with people I care about	
Told people close to me that they were important	
Apologized or made repairs when I was wrong	
Expressed appreciation and thankfulness to others	
Empathized with others or thought about problems from their perspective	
Established limits and boundaries when necessary	

TOTAL SCORE FOR THIS SECTION

SPIRITUAL CARE	SCORE
Attended religious or spiritual services	
Spent time with others who share similar beliefs	
Sought spiritual direction or guidance	
Prayed or asked someone to pray for me	
Practiced mindfulness and/or meditation	
Identified important values and sought meaning in my life	
Read or watched things that helped to inspire me	

TOTAL SCORE FOR THIS SECTION

THE WEEK AHEAD

Daily self-care tracker

		M	T	W	T	F	S	S
PHYSICAL	Exercised for at least 10–15 minutes	✓	✗					
	Took prescribed medications as directed							
	Refrained from self-medicating							
	Got enough sleep							
	Ate balanced meals							
EMOTIONAL	Skillfully tolerated distressing moments							
	Validated my own thoughts, emotions, and experiences							
	Practiced self-compassion							
	Engaged in mindful breathing or breath counting							
	Observed and described feelings mindfully							
RELATIONAL	Practiced empathy and unconditional kindness							
	Let go of judgments about others							
	Used problem-solving skills to strengthen relationships							
	Said no and established limits when necessary							
	Expressed a mindful interest in others							
SPIRITUAL	Used prayer or meditation to help myself							
	Sought or created meaning in my life							
	Allowed myself to be inspired or to inspire others							
	Honored my values and beliefs							
	Attended religious or spiritual services							

MONDAY

DATE /   /

Skills practiced

MINDFULNESS	EMOTION REGULATION	DISTRESS TOLERANCE	INTERPERSONAL EFFECTIVENESS

Things that I'm **thankful** for

1.
2.
3.

Goals I worked towards

Today's **shining moment**

Notes and reminders

DAYS SOBER OR NUMBER OF DAYS SINCE ENGAGING IN A HARMFUL OR DESTRUCTIVE BEHAVIOR	BEHAVIOR	DAYS SINCE
		☐ ☐ ☐
		☐ ☐ ☐
		☐ ☐ ☐

TUESDAY

DATE   /   /

Skills practiced

MINDFULNESS	EMOTION REGULATION	DISTRESS TOLERANCE	INTERPERSONAL EFFECTIVENESS

Things that I'm **thankful** for

1.
2.
3.

Goals I worked towards

Today's **shining moment**

Notes and reminders

DAYS SOBER
OR NUMBER OF DAYS SINCE ENGAGING IN A HARMFUL OR DESTRUCTIVE BEHAVIOR

BEHAVIOR	DAYS SINCE

WEDNESDAY

DATE   /   /

Skills practiced

MINDFULNESS	EMOTION REGULATION	DISTRESS TOLERANCE	INTERPERSONAL EFFECTIVENESS

Things that I'm **thankful** for

1.
2.
3.

Goals I worked towards

Today's **shining moment**

Notes and reminders

DAYS SOBER
OR NUMBER OF DAYS SINCE ENGAGING IN A HARMFUL OR DESTRUCTIVE BEHAVIOR

BEHAVIOR	DAYS SINCE

THURSDAY

Skills practiced

MINDFULNESS	EMOTION REGULATION	DISTRESS TOLERANCE	INTERPERSONAL EFFECTIVENESS

Things that I'm **thankful** for

1.
2.
3.

Goals I worked towards

Today's **shining moment**

Notes and reminders

DAYS SOBER
OR NUMBER OF DAYS SINCE ENGAGING IN A HARMFUL OR DESTRUCTIVE BEHAVIOR

BEHAVIOR	DAYS SINCE

FRIDAY

Skills practiced

MINDFULNESS	EMOTION REGULATION	DISTRESS TOLERANCE	INTERPERSONAL EFFECTIVENESS

Things that I'm **thankful** for

1.
2.
3.

Goals I worked towards

Today's **shining moment**

Notes and reminders

DAYS SOBER
OR NUMBER OF DAYS SINCE ENGAGING IN A HARMFUL OR DESTRUCTIVE BEHAVIOR

BEHAVIOR	DAYS SINCE

SATURDAY

DATE   /   /

Skills practiced

MINDFULNESS	EMOTION REGULATION	DISTRESS TOLERANCE	INTERPERSONAL EFFECTIVENESS

Things that I'm **thankful** for

1.
2.
3.

Goals I worked towards

Today's **shining moment**

Notes and reminders

DAYS SOBER
OR NUMBER OF DAYS SINCE ENGAGING IN A HARMFUL OR DESTRUCTIVE BEHAVIOR

BEHAVIOR	DAYS SINCE

SUNDAY

DATE   /   /

Skills practiced

MINDFULNESS	EMOTION REGULATION	DISTRESS TOLERANCE	INTERPERSONAL EFFECTIVENESS

Things that I'm **thankful** for

1.
2.
3.

Goals I worked towards

Today's **shining moment**

Notes and reminders

DAYS SOBER
OR NUMBER OF DAYS SINCE ENGAGING IN A HARMFUL OR DESTRUCTIVE BEHAVIOR

BEHAVIOR	DAYS SINCE

THE WEEK AHEAD

Daily self-care tracker

		M	T	W	T	F	S	S
PHYSICAL	Exercised for at least 10–15 minutes	✓✗						
	Took prescribed medications as directed							
	Refrained from self-medicating							
	Got enough sleep							
	Ate balanced meals							
EMOTIONAL	Skillfully tolerated distressing moments							
	Validated my own thoughts, emotions, and experiences							
	Practiced self-compassion							
	Engaged in mindful breathing or breath counting							
	Observed and described feelings mindfully							
RELATIONAL	Practiced empathy and unconditional kindness							
	Let go of judgments about others							
	Used problem-solving skills to strengthen relationships							
	Said no and established limits when necessary							
	Expressed a mindful interest in others							
SPIRITUAL	Used prayer or meditation to help myself							
	Sought or created meaning in my life							
	Allowed myself to be inspired or to inspire others							
	Honored my values and beliefs							
	Attended religious or spiritual services							

MONDAY

DATE   /   /

Skills practiced

MINDFULNESS	EMOTION REGULATION	DISTRESS TOLERANCE	INTERPERSONAL EFFECTIVENESS

Things that I'm **thankful** for

1.
2.
3.

Goals I worked towards

Today's **shining moment**

Notes and reminders

DAYS SOBER	BEHAVIOR	DAYS SINCE
OR NUMBER OF DAYS SINCE ENGAGING IN A HARMFUL OR DESTRUCTIVE BEHAVIOR		▢▢▢
		▢▢▢
		▢▢▢

TUESDAY

DATE / /

Skills practiced

MINDFULNESS	EMOTION REGULATION	DISTRESS TOLERANCE	INTERPERSONAL EFFECTIVENESS

Things that I'm **thankful** for

1.
2.
3.

Goals I worked towards

Today's **shining moment**

Notes and reminders

DAYS SOBER
OR NUMBER OF DAYS SINCE ENGAGING IN A HARMFUL OR DESTRUCTIVE BEHAVIOR

BEHAVIOR	DAYS SINCE

WEDNESDAY

DATE / /

Skills practiced

MINDFULNESS	EMOTION REGULATION	DISTRESS TOLERANCE	INTERPERSONAL EFFECTIVENESS

Things that I'm **thankful** for

1.
2.
3.

Goals I worked towards

Today's **shining moment**

Notes and reminders

DAYS SOBER
OR NUMBER OF DAYS SINCE ENGAGING IN A HARMFUL OR DESTRUCTIVE BEHAVIOR

BEHAVIOR	DAYS SINCE

THURSDAY

Skills practiced

MINDFULNESS	EMOTION REGULATION	DISTRESS TOLERANCE	INTERPERSONAL EFFECTIVENESS

Things that I'm **thankful** for

1.
2.
3.

Goals I worked towards

Today's **shining moment**

Notes and reminders

DAYS SOBER
OR NUMBER OF DAYS SINCE ENGAGING IN A HARMFUL OR DESTRUCTIVE BEHAVIOR

BEHAVIOR	DAYS SINCE

FRIDAY

DATE / /

Skills practiced

MINDFULNESS	EMOTION REGULATION	DISTRESS TOLERANCE	INTERPERSONAL EFFECTIVENESS

Things that I'm **thankful** for

1.
2.
3.

Goals I worked towards

Today's **shining moment**

Notes and reminders

DAYS SOBER
OR NUMBER OF DAYS SINCE ENGAGING IN A HARMFUL OR DESTRUCTIVE BEHAVIOR

BEHAVIOR	DAYS SINCE

SATURDAY

DATE   /   /

Skills practiced

MINDFULNESS	EMOTION REGULATION	DISTRESS TOLERANCE	INTERPERSONAL EFFECTIVENESS

Things that I'm **thankful** for

1.
2.
3.

Goals I worked towards

Today's **shining moment**

Notes and reminders

DAYS SOBER OR NUMBER OF DAYS SINCE ENGAGING IN A HARMFUL OR DESTRUCTIVE BEHAVIOR

BEHAVIOR

DAYS SINCE

SUNDAY

DATE   /   /

Skills practiced

MINDFULNESS	EMOTION REGULATION	DISTRESS TOLERANCE	INTERPERSONAL EFFECTIVENESS

Things that I'm **thankful** for

1.
2.
3.

Goals I worked towards

Today's **shining moment**

Notes and reminders

DAYS SOBER OR NUMBER OF DAYS SINCE ENGAGING IN A HARMFUL OR DESTRUCTIVE BEHAVIOR

BEHAVIOR

DAYS SINCE

THE WEEK AHEAD

Daily self-care tracker

		M	T	W	T	F	S	S
PHYSICAL	Exercised for at least 10-15 minutes	✓✗						
	Took prescribed medications as directed							
	Refrained from self-medicating							
	Got enough sleep							
	Ate balanced meals							
EMOTIONAL	Skillfully tolerated distressing moments							
	Validated my own thoughts, emotions, and experiences							
	Practiced self-compassion							
	Engaged in mindful breathing or breath counting							
	Observed and described feelings mindfully							
RELATIONAL	Practiced empathy and unconditional kindness							
	Let go of judgments about others							
	Used problem-solving skills to strengthen relationships							
	Said no and established limits when necessary							
	Expressed a mindful interest in others							
SPIRITUAL	Used prayer or meditation to help myself							
	Sought or created meaning in my life							
	Allowed myself to be inspired or to inspire others							
	Honored my values and beliefs							
	Attended religious or spiritual services							

MONDAY

DATE   /   /

Skills practiced

MINDFULNESS	EMOTION REGULATION	DISTRESS TOLERANCE	INTERPERSONAL EFFECTIVENESS

Things that I'm thankful for

1.
2.
3.

Goals I worked towards

Today's shining moment

Notes and reminders

DAYS SOBER
OR NUMBER OF DAYS SINCE ENGAGING IN A HARMFUL OR DESTRUCTIVE BEHAVIOR

BEHAVIOR	DAYS SINCE
	☐ ☐ ☐
	☐ ☐ ☐
	☐ ☐ ☐

TUESDAY

DATE / /

Skills practiced

MINDFULNESS	EMOTION REGULATION	DISTRESS TOLERANCE	INTERPERSONAL EFFECTIVENESS

Things that I'm **thankful** for

1.
2.
3.

Goals I worked towards

Today's **shining moment**

Notes and reminders

DAYS SOBER
OR NUMBER OF DAYS SINCE ENGAGING IN A HARMFUL OR DESTRUCTIVE BEHAVIOR

BEHAVIOR	DAYS SINCE

WEDNESDAY

DATE / /

Skills practiced

MINDFULNESS	EMOTION REGULATION	DISTRESS TOLERANCE	INTERPERSONAL EFFECTIVENESS

Things that I'm **thankful** for

1.
2.
3.

Goals I worked towards

Today's **shining moment**

Notes and reminders

DAYS SOBER
OR NUMBER OF DAYS SINCE ENGAGING IN A HARMFUL OR DESTRUCTIVE BEHAVIOR

BEHAVIOR	DAYS SINCE

THURSDAY

Skills practiced

MINDFULNESS	EMOTION REGULATION	DISTRESS TOLERANCE	INTERPERSONAL EFFECTIVENESS

Things that I'm **thankful** for

1.
2.
3.

Goals I worked towards

Today's **shining moment**

Notes and reminders

DAYS SOBER OR NUMBER OF DAYS SINCE ENGAGING IN A HARMFUL OR DESTRUCTIVE BEHAVIOR	BEHAVIOR	DAYS SINCE

FRIDAY

DATE   /   /

Skills practiced

MINDFULNESS	EMOTION REGULATION	DISTRESS TOLERANCE	INTERPERSONAL EFFECTIVENESS

Things that I'm **thankful** for

1.
2.
3.

Goals I worked towards

Today's **shining moment**

Notes and reminders

DAYS SOBER OR NUMBER OF DAYS SINCE ENGAGING IN A HARMFUL OR DESTRUCTIVE BEHAVIOR	BEHAVIOR	DAYS SINCE

SATURDAY

DATE   /   /

Skills practiced

MINDFULNESS	EMOTION REGULATION	DISTRESS TOLERANCE	INTERPERSONAL EFFECTIVENESS

Things that I'm **thankful** for

1.
2.
3.

Goals I worked towards

Today's **shining moment**

Notes and reminders

DAYS SOBER
OR NUMBER OF DAYS SINCE ENGAGING IN A HARMFUL OR DESTRUCTIVE BEHAVIOR

BEHAVIOR	DAYS SINCE

SUNDAY

DATE   /   /

Skills practiced

MINDFULNESS	EMOTION REGULATION	DISTRESS TOLERANCE	INTERPERSONAL EFFECTIVENESS

Things that I'm **thankful** for

1.
2.
3.

Goals I worked towards

Today's **shining moment**

Notes and reminders

DAYS SOBER
OR NUMBER OF DAYS SINCE ENGAGING IN A HARMFUL OR DESTRUCTIVE BEHAVIOR

BEHAVIOR	DAYS SINCE

THE WEEK AHEAD

Daily self-care tracker

		M	T	W	T	F	S	S
PHYSICAL	Exercised for at least 10–15 minutes	✓/✗						
	Took prescribed medications as directed							
	Refrained from self-medicating							
	Got enough sleep							
	Ate balanced meals							
EMOTIONAL	Skillfully tolerated distressing moments							
	Validated my own thoughts, emotions, and experiences							
	Practiced self-compassion							
	Engaged in mindful breathing or breath counting							
	Observed and described feelings mindfully							
RELATIONAL	Practiced empathy and unconditional kindness							
	Let go of judgments about others							
	Used problem-solving skills to strengthen relationships							
	Said no and established limits when necessary							
	Expressed a mindful interest in others							
SPIRITUAL	Used prayer or meditation to help myself							
	Sought or created meaning in my life							
	Allowed myself to be inspired or to inspire others							
	Honored my values and beliefs							
	Attended religious or spiritual services							

MONDAY

DATE   /   /

Skills practiced

MINDFULNESS	EMOTION REGULATION	DISTRESS TOLERANCE	INTERPERSONAL EFFECTIVENESS

Things that I'm **thankful** for

1.
2.
3.

Goals I worked towards

Today's **shining moment**

Notes and reminders

DAYS SOBER
OR NUMBER OF DAYS SINCE ENGAGING IN A HARMFUL OR DESTRUCTIVE BEHAVIOR

BEHAVIOR	DAYS SINCE
	☐☐☐
	☐☐☐
	☐☐☐

TUESDAY

DATE / /

Skills practiced

MINDFULNESS	EMOTION REGULATION	DISTRESS TOLERANCE	INTERPERSONAL EFFECTIVENESS

Things that I'm **thankful** for

1.
2.
3.

Goals I worked towards

Today's **shining moment**

Notes and reminders

DAYS SOBER OR NUMBER OF DAYS SINCE ENGAGING IN A HARMFUL OR DESTRUCTIVE BEHAVIOR	BEHAVIOR	DAYS SINCE

WEDNESDAY

DATE / /

Skills practiced

MINDFULNESS	EMOTION REGULATION	DISTRESS TOLERANCE	INTERPERSONAL EFFECTIVENESS

Things that I'm **thankful** for

1.
2.
3.

Goals I worked towards

Today's **shining moment**

Notes and reminders

DAYS SOBER OR NUMBER OF DAYS SINCE ENGAGING IN A HARMFUL OR DESTRUCTIVE BEHAVIOR	BEHAVIOR	DAYS SINCE

THURSDAY

Skills practiced

MINDFULNESS	EMOTION REGULATION	DISTRESS TOLERANCE	INTERPERSONAL EFFECTIVENESS

Things that I'm **thankful** for

1.
2.
3.

Goals I worked towards

Today's **shining moment**

Notes and reminders

DAYS SOBER OR NUMBER OF DAYS SINCE ENGAGING IN A HARMFUL OR DESTRUCTIVE BEHAVIOR

BEHAVIOR	DAYS SINCE

FRIDAY

Skills practiced

MINDFULNESS	EMOTION REGULATION	DISTRESS TOLERANCE	INTERPERSONAL EFFECTIVENESS

Things that I'm **thankful** for

1.
2.
3.

Goals I worked towards

Today's **shining moment**

Notes and reminders

DAYS SOBER OR NUMBER OF DAYS SINCE ENGAGING IN A HARMFUL OR DESTRUCTIVE BEHAVIOR

BEHAVIOR	DAYS SINCE

SATURDAY

DATE / /

Skills practiced

MINDFULNESS	EMOTION REGULATION	DISTRESS TOLERANCE	INTERPERSONAL EFFECTIVENESS

Things that I'm **thankful** for

1.
2.
3.

Goals I worked towards

Today's **shining moment**

Notes and reminders

DAYS SOBER OR NUMBER OF DAYS SINCE ENGAGING IN A HARMFUL OR DESTRUCTIVE BEHAVIOR

BEHAVIOR	DAYS SINCE

SUNDAY

DATE / /

Skills practiced

MINDFULNESS	EMOTION REGULATION	DISTRESS TOLERANCE	INTERPERSONAL EFFECTIVENESS

Things that I'm **thankful** for

1.
2.
3.

Goals I worked towards

Today's **shining moment**

Notes and reminders

DAYS SOBER OR NUMBER OF DAYS SINCE ENGAGING IN A HARMFUL OR DESTRUCTIVE BEHAVIOR

BEHAVIOR	DAYS SINCE

SELF-CARE ASSESSMENT

Over the past 28 days, how often have you engaged in these specific self-care methods?

SCORING	
4	**Always**
3	**Often**
2	**Sometimes**
1	**Rarely**
0	Not applicable to me at this time

PHYSICAL CARE	SCORE
Ate small balanced meals throughout the day	
Exercised for at least 15–20 minutes each day	
Followed preventive care instructions	
Bathed and brushed teeth daily	
Balanced sleep	
Refrained from self-medicating with alcohol, drugs, or prescription medicine	
Treated illness promptly	

TOTAL SCORE FOR THIS SECTION

EMOTIONAL CARE	SCORE
Attended all scheduled treatment and therapy appointments	
Made time for hobbies and enjoyable activities	
Politely said no to unwanted requests	
Let others know when I needed extra help	
Spent time with friends and loved ones	
Validated my own emotions, thoughts, and experiences	
Practiced self-compassion	

TOTAL SCORE FOR THIS SECTION

TOTAL SCORE PER SECTION

20-28	**Excellent!** You're doing a great job of taking care of yourself in this area.
11-19	**Very good.** Identify and address any gaps in self-care.
Below 10	**No one is perfect.** Is this an area of growth for you?

Remember, a score of zero (not applicable) in any area may lower your section score.

RELATIONAL CARE	SCORE
Stayed connected to friends and family members	
Set aside time to spend with people I care about	
Told people close to me that they were important	
Apologized or made repairs when I was wrong	
Expressed appreciation and thankfulness to others	
Empathized with others or thought about problems from their perspective	
Established limits and boundaries when necessary	

TOTAL SCORE FOR THIS SECTION

SPIRITUAL CARE	SCORE
Attended religious or spiritual services	
Spent time with others who share similar beliefs	
Sought spiritual direction or guidance	
Prayed or asked someone to pray for me	
Practiced mindfulness and/or meditation	
Identified important values and sought meaning in my life	
Read or watched things that helped to inspire me	

TOTAL SCORE FOR THIS SECTION

THE WEEK AHEAD

Daily self-care tracker

		M	T	W	T	F	S	S
PHYSICAL	Exercised for at least 10-15 minutes	✓/✗						
	Took prescribed medications as directed							
	Refrained from self-medicating							
	Got enough sleep							
	Ate balanced meals							
EMOTIONAL	Skillfully tolerated distressing moments							
	Validated my own thoughts, emotions, and experiences							
	Practiced self-compassion							
	Engaged in mindful breathing or breath counting							
	Observed and described feelings mindfully							
RELATIONAL	Practiced empathy and unconditional kindness							
	Let go of judgments about others							
	Used problem-solving skills to strengthen relationships							
	Said no and established limits when necessary							
	Expressed a mindful interest in others							
SPIRITUAL	Used prayer or meditation to help myself							
	Sought or created meaning in my life							
	Allowed myself to be inspired or to inspire others							
	Honored my values and beliefs							
	Attended religious or spiritual services							

MONDAY

DATE / /

Skills practiced

MINDFULNESS	EMOTION REGULATION	DISTRESS TOLERANCE	INTERPERSONAL EFFECTIVENESS

Things that I'm thankful for

1.

2.

3.

Goals I worked towards

Today's shining moment

Notes and reminders

DAYS SOBER
OR NUMBER OF DAYS SINCE ENGAGING IN A HARMFUL OR DESTRUCTIVE BEHAVIOR

BEHAVIOR	DAYS SINCE
	☐☐☐
	☐☐☐
	☐☐☐

TUESDAY

DATE / /

Skills practiced

MINDFULNESS	EMOTION REGULATION	DISTRESS TOLERANCE	INTERPERSONAL EFFECTIVENESS

Things that I'm **thankful** for

1.
2.
3.

Goals I worked towards

Today's **shining moment**

Notes and reminders

DAYS SOBER OR NUMBER OF DAYS SINCE ENGAGING IN A HARMFUL OR DESTRUCTIVE BEHAVIOR

BEHAVIOR	DAYS SINCE

WEDNESDAY

DATE / /

Skills practiced

MINDFULNESS	EMOTION REGULATION	DISTRESS TOLERANCE	INTERPERSONAL EFFECTIVENESS

Things that I'm **thankful** for

1.
2.
3.

Goals I worked towards

Today's **shining moment**

Notes and reminders

DAYS SOBER OR NUMBER OF DAYS SINCE ENGAGING IN A HARMFUL OR DESTRUCTIVE BEHAVIOR

BEHAVIOR	DAYS SINCE

THURSDAY

DATE   /   /

Skills practiced

MINDFULNESS	EMOTION REGULATION	DISTRESS TOLERANCE	INTERPERSONAL EFFECTIVENESS

Things that I'm **thankful** for

1.

2.

3.

Goals I worked towards

Today's **shining moment**

Notes and reminders

DAYS SOBER OR NUMBER OF DAYS SINCE ENGAGING IN A HARMFUL OR DESTRUCTIVE BEHAVIOR	BEHAVIOR	DAYS SINCE

FRIDAY

DATE   /   /

Skills practiced

MINDFULNESS	EMOTION REGULATION	DISTRESS TOLERANCE	INTERPERSONAL EFFECTIVENESS

Things that I'm **thankful** for

1.

2.

3.

Goals I worked towards

Today's **shining moment**

Notes and reminders

DAYS SOBER OR NUMBER OF DAYS SINCE ENGAGING IN A HARMFUL OR DESTRUCTIVE BEHAVIOR	BEHAVIOR	DAYS SINCE

SATURDAY

DATE   /   /

Skills practiced

MINDFULNESS	EMOTION REGULATION	DISTRESS TOLERANCE	INTERPERSONAL EFFECTIVENESS

Things that I'm **thankful** for

1.
2.
3.

Goals I worked towards

Today's **shining moment**

Notes and reminders

DAYS SOBER OR NUMBER OF DAYS SINCE ENGAGING IN A HARMFUL OR DESTRUCTIVE BEHAVIOR

BEHAVIOR	DAYS SINCE

SUNDAY

DATE   /   /

Skills practiced

MINDFULNESS	EMOTION REGULATION	DISTRESS TOLERANCE	INTERPERSONAL EFFECTIVENESS

Things that I'm **thankful** for

1.
2.
3.

Goals I worked towards

Today's **shining moment**

Notes and reminders

DAYS SOBER OR NUMBER OF DAYS SINCE ENGAGING IN A HARMFUL OR DESTRUCTIVE BEHAVIOR

BEHAVIOR	DAYS SINCE

THE WEEK AHEAD

Daily self-care tracker

		M	T	W	T	F	S	S
PHYSICAL	Exercised for at least 10–15 minutes	✓/✗						
	Took prescribed medications as directed							
	Refrained from self-medicating							
	Got enough sleep							
	Ate balanced meals							
EMOTIONAL	Skillfully tolerated distressing moments							
	Validated my own thoughts, emotions, and experiences							
	Practiced self-compassion							
	Engaged in mindful breathing or breath counting							
	Observed and described feelings mindfully							
RELATIONAL	Practiced empathy and unconditional kindness							
	Let go of judgments about others							
	Used problem-solving skills to strengthen relationships							
	Said no and established limits when necessary							
	Expressed a mindful interest in others							
SPIRITUAL	Used prayer or meditation to help myself							
	Sought or created meaning in my life							
	Allowed myself to be inspired or to inspire others							
	Honored my values and beliefs							
	Attended religious or spiritual services							

MONDAY

DATE / /

Skills practiced

MINDFULNESS	EMOTION REGULATION	DISTRESS TOLERANCE	INTERPERSONAL EFFECTIVENESS

Things that I'm **thankful** for

1.

2.

3.

Goals I worked towards

Today's **shining moment**

Notes and reminders

DAYS SOBER

OR NUMBER OF DAYS SINCE ENGAGING IN A HARMFUL OR DESTRUCTIVE BEHAVIOR

BEHAVIOR	DAYS SINCE
	☐ ☐ ☐
	☐ ☐ ☐
	☐ ☐ ☐

TUESDAY

DATE / /

Skills practiced

MINDFULNESS	EMOTION REGULATION	DISTRESS TOLERANCE	INTERPERSONAL EFFECTIVENESS

Things that I'm **thankful** for

1.
2.
3.

Goals I worked towards

Today's **shining moment**

Notes and reminders

DAYS SOBER OR NUMBER OF DAYS SINCE ENGAGING IN A HARMFUL OR DESTRUCTIVE BEHAVIOR

BEHAVIOR	DAYS SINCE

WEDNESDAY

DATE / /

Skills practiced

MINDFULNESS	EMOTION REGULATION	DISTRESS TOLERANCE	INTERPERSONAL EFFECTIVENESS

Things that I'm **thankful** for

1.
2.
3.

Goals I worked towards

Today's **shining moment**

Notes and reminders

DAYS SOBER OR NUMBER OF DAYS SINCE ENGAGING IN A HARMFUL OR DESTRUCTIVE BEHAVIOR

BEHAVIOR	DAYS SINCE

THURSDAY

Skills practiced

MINDFULNESS	EMOTION REGULATION	DISTRESS TOLERANCE	INTERPERSONAL EFFECTIVENESS

Things that I'm **thankful** for

1.
2.
3.

Goals I worked towards

Today's **shining moment**

Notes and reminders

DAYS SOBER OR NUMBER OF DAYS SINCE ENGAGING IN A HARMFUL OR DESTRUCTIVE BEHAVIOR	BEHAVIOR	DAYS SINCE
		☐ ☐ ☐
		☐ ☐ ☐
		☐ ☐ ☐

FRIDAY

Skills practiced

MINDFULNESS	EMOTION REGULATION	DISTRESS TOLERANCE	INTERPERSONAL EFFECTIVENESS

Things that I'm **thankful** for

1.
2.
3.

Goals I worked towards

Today's **shining moment**

Notes and reminders

DAYS SOBER OR NUMBER OF DAYS SINCE ENGAGING IN A HARMFUL OR DESTRUCTIVE BEHAVIOR	BEHAVIOR	DAYS SINCE
		☐ ☐ ☐
		☐ ☐ ☐
		☐ ☐ ☐

SATURDAY

DATE / /

Skills practiced

MINDFULNESS	EMOTION REGULATION	DISTRESS TOLERANCE	INTERPERSONAL EFFECTIVENESS

Things that I'm **thankful** for

1.
2.
3.

Goals I worked towards

Today's **shining moment**

Notes and reminders

DAYS SOBER
OR NUMBER OF DAYS SINCE ENGAGING IN A HARMFUL OR DESTRUCTIVE BEHAVIOR

BEHAVIOR	DAYS SINCE

SUNDAY

DATE / /

Skills practiced

MINDFULNESS	EMOTION REGULATION	DISTRESS TOLERANCE	INTERPERSONAL EFFECTIVENESS

Things that I'm **thankful** for

1.
2.
3.

Goals I worked towards

Today's **shining moment**

Notes and reminders

DAYS SOBER
OR NUMBER OF DAYS SINCE ENGAGING IN A HARMFUL OR DESTRUCTIVE BEHAVIOR

BEHAVIOR	DAYS SINCE

THE WEEK AHEAD

Daily self-care tracker

		M	T	W	T	F	S	S
PHYSICAL	Exercised for at least 10-15 minutes	✓/✗						
	Took prescribed medications as directed							
	Refrained from self-medicating							
	Got enough sleep							
	Ate balanced meals							
EMOTIONAL	Skillfully tolerated distressing moments							
	Validated my own thoughts, emotions, and experiences							
	Practiced self-compassion							
	Engaged in mindful breathing or breath counting							
	Observed and described feelings mindfully							
RELATIONAL	Practiced empathy and unconditional kindness							
	Let go of judgments about others							
	Used problem-solving skills to strengthen relationships							
	Said no and established limits when necessary							
	Expressed a mindful interest in others							
SPIRITUAL	Used prayer or meditation to help myself							
	Sought or created meaning in my life							
	Allowed myself to be inspired or to inspire others							
	Honored my values and beliefs							
	Attended religious or spiritual services							

MONDAY

DATE   /   /

Skills practiced

MINDFULNESS	EMOTION REGULATION	DISTRESS TOLERANCE	INTERPERSONAL EFFECTIVENESS

Things that I'm **thankful** for

1.
2.
3.

Goals I worked towards

Today's **shining moment**

Notes and reminders

DAYS SOBER
OR NUMBER OF DAYS SINCE ENGAGING IN A HARMFUL OR DESTRUCTIVE BEHAVIOR

BEHAVIOR	DAYS SINCE
	☐ ☐ ☐
	☐ ☐ ☐
	☐ ☐ ☐

TUESDAY

DATE ___ / ___ / ___

Skills practiced

MINDFULNESS	EMOTION REGULATION	DISTRESS TOLERANCE	INTERPERSONAL EFFECTIVENESS

Things that I'm **thankful** for

1.
2.
3.

Goals I worked towards

Today's **shining moment**

Notes and reminders

DAYS SOBER OR NUMBER OF DAYS SINCE ENGAGING IN A HARMFUL OR DESTRUCTIVE BEHAVIOR

BEHAVIOR	DAYS SINCE

WEDNESDAY

DATE ___ / ___ / ___

Skills practiced

MINDFULNESS	EMOTION REGULATION	DISTRESS TOLERANCE	INTERPERSONAL EFFECTIVENESS

Things that I'm **thankful** for

1.
2.
3.

Goals I worked towards

Today's **shining moment**

Notes and reminders

DAYS SOBER OR NUMBER OF DAYS SINCE ENGAGING IN A HARMFUL OR DESTRUCTIVE BEHAVIOR

BEHAVIOR	DAYS SINCE

THURSDAY

DATE / /

Skills practiced

MINDFULNESS	EMOTION REGULATION	DISTRESS TOLERANCE	INTERPERSONAL EFFECTIVENESS

Things that I'm **thankful** for

1.
2.
3.

Goals I worked towards

Today's **shining moment**

Notes and reminders

DAYS SOBER OR NUMBER OF DAYS SINCE ENGAGING IN A HARMFUL OR DESTRUCTIVE BEHAVIOR

BEHAVIOR	DAYS SINCE

FRIDAY

DATE / /

Skills practiced

MINDFULNESS	EMOTION REGULATION	DISTRESS TOLERANCE	INTERPERSONAL EFFECTIVENESS

Things that I'm **thankful** for

1.
2.
3.

Goals I worked towards

Today's **shining moment**

Notes and reminders

DAYS SOBER OR NUMBER OF DAYS SINCE ENGAGING IN A HARMFUL OR DESTRUCTIVE BEHAVIOR

BEHAVIOR	DAYS SINCE

SATURDAY

Skills practiced

MINDFULNESS	EMOTION REGULATION	DISTRESS TOLERANCE	INTERPERSONAL EFFECTIVENESS

Things that I'm **thankful** for

1.
2.
3.

Goals I worked towards

Today's **shining moment**

Notes and reminders

DAYS SOBER
OR NUMBER OF DAYS SINCE ENGAGING IN A HARMFUL OR DESTRUCTIVE BEHAVIOR

BEHAVIOR	DAYS SINCE

SUNDAY

DATE   /   /

Skills practiced

MINDFULNESS	EMOTION REGULATION	DISTRESS TOLERANCE	INTERPERSONAL EFFECTIVENESS

Things that I'm **thankful** for

1.
2.
3.

Goals I worked towards

Today's **shining moment**

Notes and reminders

DAYS SOBER
OR NUMBER OF DAYS SINCE ENGAGING IN A HARMFUL OR DESTRUCTIVE BEHAVIOR

BEHAVIOR	DAYS SINCE

THE WEEK AHEAD

Daily self-care tracker

		M	T	W	T	F	S	S
PHYSICAL	Exercised for at least 10–15 minutes							
	Took prescribed medications as directed							
	Refrained from self-medicating							
	Got enough sleep							
	Ate balanced meals							
EMOTIONAL	Skillfully tolerated distressing moments							
	Validated my own thoughts, emotions, and experiences							
	Practiced self-compassion							
	Engaged in mindful breathing or breath counting							
	Observed and described feelings mindfully							
RELATIONAL	Practiced empathy and unconditional kindness							
	Let go of judgments about others							
	Used problem-solving skills to strengthen relationships							
	Said no and established limits when necessary							
	Expressed a mindful interest in others							
SPIRITUAL	Used prayer or meditation to help myself							
	Sought or created meaning in my life							
	Allowed myself to be inspired or to inspire others							
	Honored my values and beliefs							
	Attended religious or spiritual services							

MONDAY

DATE   /   /

Skills practiced

MINDFULNESS	EMOTION REGULATION	DISTRESS TOLERANCE	INTERPERSONAL EFFECTIVENESS

Things that I'm **thankful** for

1.
2.
3.

Goals I worked towards

Today's **shining moment**

Notes and reminders

DAYS SOBER	BEHAVIOR	DAYS SINCE
OR NUMBER OF DAYS SINCE ENGAGING IN A HARMFUL OR DESTRUCTIVE BEHAVIOR		

TUESDAY

DATE   /   /

Skills practiced

MINDFULNESS	EMOTION REGULATION	DISTRESS TOLERANCE	INTERPERSONAL EFFECTIVENESS

Things that I'm thankful for

1.
2.
3.

Goals I worked towards

Today's shining moment

Notes and reminders

DAYS SOBER OR NUMBER OF DAYS SINCE ENGAGING IN A HARMFUL OR DESTRUCTIVE BEHAVIOR	BEHAVIOR	DAYS SINCE

WEDNESDAY

DATE   /   /

Skills practiced

MINDFULNESS	EMOTION REGULATION	DISTRESS TOLERANCE	INTERPERSONAL EFFECTIVENESS

Things that I'm thankful for

1.
2.
3.

Goals I worked towards

Today's shining moment

Notes and reminders

DAYS SOBER OR NUMBER OF DAYS SINCE ENGAGING IN A HARMFUL OR DESTRUCTIVE BEHAVIOR	BEHAVIOR	DAYS SINCE

THURSDAY

Skills practiced

MINDFULNESS	EMOTION REGULATION	DISTRESS TOLERANCE	INTERPERSONAL EFFECTIVENESS

Things that I'm **thankful** for

1.
2.
3.

Goals I worked towards

Today's **shining moment**

Notes and reminders

DAYS SOBER
OR NUMBER OF DAYS SINCE ENGAGING IN A HARMFUL OR DESTRUCTIVE BEHAVIOR

BEHAVIOR	DAYS SINCE

FRIDAY

DATE / /

Skills practiced

MINDFULNESS	EMOTION REGULATION	DISTRESS TOLERANCE	INTERPERSONAL EFFECTIVENESS

Things that I'm **thankful** for

1.
2.
3.

Goals I worked towards

Today's **shining moment**

Notes and reminders

DAYS SOBER
OR NUMBER OF DAYS SINCE ENGAGING IN A HARMFUL OR DESTRUCTIVE BEHAVIOR

BEHAVIOR	DAYS SINCE

SATURDAY

Skills practiced

MINDFULNESS	EMOTION REGULATION	DISTRESS TOLERANCE	INTERPERSONAL EFFECTIVENESS

Things that I'm **thankful** for

1.
2.
3.

Goals I worked towards

Today's **shining moment**

Notes and reminders

DAYS SOBER
OR NUMBER OF DAYS SINCE ENGAGING IN A HARMFUL OR DESTRUCTIVE BEHAVIOR

BEHAVIOR	DAYS SINCE

SUNDAY

DATE / /

Skills practiced

MINDFULNESS	EMOTION REGULATION	DISTRESS TOLERANCE	INTERPERSONAL EFFECTIVENESS

Things that I'm **thankful** for

1.
2.
3.

Goals I worked towards

Today's **shining moment**

Notes and reminders

DAYS SOBER
OR NUMBER OF DAYS SINCE ENGAGING IN A HARMFUL OR DESTRUCTIVE BEHAVIOR

BEHAVIOR	DAYS SINCE

SELF-CARE ASSESSMENT

Over the past 28 days, how often have you engaged in these specific self-care methods?

PHYSICAL CARE	SCORE
Ate small balanced meals throughout the day	
Exercised for at least 15-20 minutes each day	
Followed preventive care instructions	
Bathed and brushed teeth daily	
Balanced sleep	
Refrained from self-medicating with alcohol, drugs, or prescription medicine	
Treated illness promptly	

TOTAL SCORE FOR THIS SECTION

EMOTIONAL CARE	SCORE
Attended all scheduled treatment and therapy appointments	
Made time for hobbies and enjoyable activities	
Politely said no to unwanted requests	
Let others know when I needed extra help	
Spent time with friends and loved ones	
Validated my own emotions, thoughts, and experiences	
Practiced self-compassion	

TOTAL SCORE FOR THIS SECTION

TOTAL SCORE PER SECTION

20-28	**Excellent!** You're doing a great job of taking care of yourself in this area.
11-19	**Very good.** Identify and address any gaps in self-care.
Below 10	**No one is perfect.** Is this an area of growth for you?

Remember, a score of zero (not applicable) in any area may lower your section score.

RELATIONAL CARE	SCORE
Stayed connected to friends and family members	
Set aside time to spend with people I care about	
Told people close to me that they were important	
Apologized or made repairs when I was wrong	
Expressed appreciation and thankfulness to others	
Empathized with others or thought about problems from their perspective	
Established limits and boundaries when necessary	

TOTAL SCORE FOR THIS SECTION

SPIRITUAL CARE	SCORE
Attended religious or spiritual services	
Spent time with others who share similar beliefs	
Sought spiritual direction or guidance	
Prayed or asked someone to pray for me	
Practiced mindfulness and/or meditation	
Identified important values and sought meaning in my life	
Read or watched things that helped to inspire me	

TOTAL SCORE FOR THIS SECTION

THE WEEK AHEAD

Daily self-care tracker

		M	T	W	T	F	S	S
PHYSICAL	Exercised for at least 10-15 minutes	✓	✗					
	Took prescribed medications as directed							
	Refrained from self-medicating							
	Got enough sleep							
	Ate balanced meals							
EMOTIONAL	Skillfully tolerated distressing moments							
	Validated my own thoughts, emotions, and experiences							
	Practiced self-compassion							
	Engaged in mindful breathing or breath counting							
	Observed and described feelings mindfully							
RELATIONAL	Practiced empathy and unconditional kindness							
	Let go of judgments about others							
	Used problem-solving skills to strengthen relationships							
	Said no and established limits when necessary							
	Expressed a mindful interest in others							
SPIRITUAL	Used prayer or meditation to help myself							
	Sought or created meaning in my life							
	Allowed myself to be inspired or to inspire others							
	Honored my values and beliefs							
	Attended religious or spiritual services							

MONDAY

DATE   /   /

Skills practiced

MINDFULNESS	EMOTION REGULATION	DISTRESS TOLERANCE	INTERPERSONAL EFFECTIVENESS

Things that I'm **thankful** for

1.
2.
3.

Goals I worked towards

Today's **shining moment**

Notes and reminders

DAYS SOBER
OR NUMBER OF DAYS SINCE ENGAGING IN A HARMFUL OR DESTRUCTIVE BEHAVIOR

BEHAVIOR	DAYS SINCE

TUESDAY

DATE   /   /

Skills practiced

MINDFULNESS	EMOTION REGULATION	DISTRESS TOLERANCE	INTERPERSONAL EFFECTIVENESS

Things that I'm **thankful** for

1.
2.
3.

Goals I worked towards

Today's **shining moment**

Notes and reminders

DAYS SOBER OR NUMBER OF DAYS SINCE ENGAGING IN A HARMFUL OR DESTRUCTIVE BEHAVIOR	BEHAVIOR	DAYS SINCE

WEDNESDAY

DATE   /   /

Skills practiced

MINDFULNESS	EMOTION REGULATION	DISTRESS TOLERANCE	INTERPERSONAL EFFECTIVENESS

Things that I'm **thankful** for

1.
2.
3.

Goals I worked towards

Today's **shining moment**

Notes and reminders

DAYS SOBER OR NUMBER OF DAYS SINCE ENGAGING IN A HARMFUL OR DESTRUCTIVE BEHAVIOR	BEHAVIOR	DAYS SINCE

THURSDAY

Skills practiced

MINDFULNESS	EMOTION REGULATION	DISTRESS TOLERANCE	INTERPERSONAL EFFECTIVENESS

Things that I'm **thankful** for

1.

2.

3.

Goals I worked towards

Today's **shining moment**

Notes and reminders

DAYS SOBER
OR NUMBER OF DAYS SINCE ENGAGING IN A HARMFUL OR DESTRUCTIVE BEHAVIOR

BEHAVIOR		DAYS SINCE

FRIDAY

Skills practiced

MINDFULNESS	EMOTION REGULATION	DISTRESS TOLERANCE	INTERPERSONAL EFFECTIVENESS

Things that I'm **thankful** for

1.

2.

3.

Goals I worked towards

Today's **shining moment**

Notes and reminders

DAYS SOBER
OR NUMBER OF DAYS SINCE ENGAGING IN A HARMFUL OR DESTRUCTIVE BEHAVIOR

BEHAVIOR		DAYS SINCE

SATURDAY

DATE   /   /

Skills practiced

MINDFULNESS	EMOTION REGULATION	DISTRESS TOLERANCE	INTERPERSONAL EFFECTIVENESS

Things that I'm **thankful** for

1.
2.
3.

Goals I worked towards

Today's **shining moment**

Notes and reminders

DAYS SOBER OR NUMBER OF DAYS SINCE ENGAGING IN A HARMFUL OR DESTRUCTIVE BEHAVIOR

BEHAVIOR	DAYS SINCE

SUNDAY

DATE   /   /

Skills practiced

MINDFULNESS	EMOTION REGULATION	DISTRESS TOLERANCE	INTERPERSONAL EFFECTIVENESS

Things that I'm **thankful** for

1.
2.
3.

Goals I worked towards

Today's **shining moment**

Notes and reminders

DAYS SOBER OR NUMBER OF DAYS SINCE ENGAGING IN A HARMFUL OR DESTRUCTIVE BEHAVIOR

BEHAVIOR	DAYS SINCE

THE WEEK AHEAD

Daily self-care tracker

		M	T	W	T	F	S	S
PHYSICAL	Exercised for at least 10-15 minutes	✓/✗						
	Took prescribed medications as directed							
	Refrained from self-medicating							
	Got enough sleep							
	Ate balanced meals							
EMOTIONAL	Skillfully tolerated distressing moments							
	Validated my own thoughts, emotions, and experiences							
	Practiced self-compassion							
	Engaged in mindful breathing or breath counting							
	Observed and described feelings mindfully							
RELATIONAL	Practiced empathy and unconditional kindness							
	Let go of judgments about others							
	Used problem-solving skills to strengthen relationships							
	Said no and established limits when necessary							
	Expressed a mindful interest in others							
SPIRITUAL	Used prayer or meditation to help myself							
	Sought or created meaning in my life							
	Allowed myself to be inspired or to inspire others							
	Honored my values and beliefs							
	Attended religious or spiritual services							

MONDAY

DATE   /   /

Skills practiced

MINDFULNESS	EMOTION REGULATION	DISTRESS TOLERANCE	INTERPERSONAL EFFECTIVENESS

Things that I'm **thankful** for

1.

2.

3.

Goals I worked towards

Today's **shining moment**

Notes and reminders

DAYS SOBER	BEHAVIOR	DAYS SINCE
OR NUMBER OF DAYS SINCE ENGAGING IN A HARMFUL OR DESTRUCTIVE BEHAVIOR		☐☐
		☐☐
		☐☐

TUESDAY

Skills practiced

MINDFULNESS	EMOTION REGULATION	DISTRESS TOLERANCE	INTERPERSONAL EFFECTIVENESS

Things that I'm **thankful** for

1.
2.
3.

Goals I worked towards

Today's **shining moment**

Notes and reminders

DAYS SOBER
OR NUMBER OF DAYS SINCE ENGAGING IN A HARMFUL OR DESTRUCTIVE BEHAVIOR

BEHAVIOR	DAYS SINCE

WEDNESDAY

DATE / /

Skills practiced

MINDFULNESS	EMOTION REGULATION	DISTRESS TOLERANCE	INTERPERSONAL EFFECTIVENESS

Things that I'm **thankful** for

1.
2.
3.

Goals I worked towards

Today's **shining moment**

Notes and reminders

DAYS SOBER
OR NUMBER OF DAYS SINCE ENGAGING IN A HARMFUL OR DESTRUCTIVE BEHAVIOR

BEHAVIOR	DAYS SINCE

THURSDAY

Skills practiced

MINDFULNESS	EMOTION REGULATION	DISTRESS TOLERANCE	INTERPERSONAL EFFECTIVENESS

Things that I'm **thankful** for

1.
2.
3.

Goals I worked towards

Today's **shining moment**

Notes and reminders

DAYS SOBER OR NUMBER OF DAYS SINCE ENGAGING IN A HARMFUL OR DESTRUCTIVE BEHAVIOR

BEHAVIOR	DAYS SINCE

FRIDAY

Skills practiced

MINDFULNESS	EMOTION REGULATION	DISTRESS TOLERANCE	INTERPERSONAL EFFECTIVENESS

Things that I'm **thankful** for

1.
2.
3.

Goals I worked towards

Today's **shining moment**

Notes and reminders

DAYS SOBER OR NUMBER OF DAYS SINCE ENGAGING IN A HARMFUL OR DESTRUCTIVE BEHAVIOR

BEHAVIOR	DAYS SINCE

SATURDAY

Skills practiced

MINDFULNESS	EMOTION REGULATION	DISTRESS TOLERANCE	INTERPERSONAL EFFECTIVENESS

Things that I'm **thankful** for

1.
2.
3.

Goals I worked towards

Today's **shining moment**

Notes and reminders

DAYS SOBER OR NUMBER OF DAYS SINCE ENGAGING IN A HARMFUL OR DESTRUCTIVE BEHAVIOR

BEHAVIOR			DAYS SINCE		

SUNDAY

Skills practiced

MINDFULNESS	EMOTION REGULATION	DISTRESS TOLERANCE	INTERPERSONAL EFFECTIVENESS

Things that I'm **thankful** for

1.
2.
3.

Goals I worked towards

Today's **shining moment**

Notes and reminders

DAYS SOBER OR NUMBER OF DAYS SINCE ENGAGING IN A HARMFUL OR DESTRUCTIVE BEHAVIOR

BEHAVIOR			DAYS SINCE		

THE WEEK AHEAD

Daily self-care tracker

		M	T	W	T	F	S	S
PHYSICAL	Exercised for at least 10–15 minutes	✓/✗						
	Took prescribed medications as directed							
	Refrained from self-medicating							
	Got enough sleep							
	Ate balanced meals							
EMOTIONAL	Skillfully tolerated distressing moments							
	Validated my own thoughts, emotions, and experiences							
	Practiced self-compassion							
	Engaged in mindful breathing or breath counting							
	Observed and described feelings mindfully							
RELATIONAL	Practiced empathy and unconditional kindness							
	Let go of judgments about others							
	Used problem-solving skills to strengthen relationships							
	Said no and established limits when necessary							
	Expressed a mindful interest in others							
SPIRITUAL	Used prayer or meditation to help myself							
	Sought or created meaning in my life							
	Allowed myself to be inspired or to inspire others							
	Honored my values and beliefs							
	Attended religious or spiritual services							

MONDAY

DATE   /   /

Skills practiced

MINDFULNESS	EMOTION REGULATION	DISTRESS TOLERANCE	INTERPERSONAL EFFECTIVENESS

Things that I'm **thankful** for

1.

2.

3.

Goals I worked towards

Today's **shining moment**

Notes and reminders

DAYS SOBER
OR NUMBER OF DAYS SINCE ENGAGING IN A HARMFUL OR DESTRUCTIVE BEHAVIOR

BEHAVIOR	DAYS SINCE

TUESDAY

DATE   /   /

Skills practiced

MINDFULNESS	EMOTION REGULATION	DISTRESS TOLERANCE	INTERPERSONAL EFFECTIVENESS

Things that I'm **thankful** for

1.
2.
3.

Goals I worked towards

Today's **shining moment**

Notes and reminders

DAYS SOBER OR NUMBER OF DAYS SINCE ENGAGING IN A HARMFUL OR DESTRUCTIVE BEHAVIOR

BEHAVIOR	DAYS SINCE

WEDNESDAY

DATE   /   /

Skills practiced

MINDFULNESS	EMOTION REGULATION	DISTRESS TOLERANCE	INTERPERSONAL EFFECTIVENESS

Things that I'm **thankful** for

1.
2.
3.

Goals I worked towards

Today's **shining moment**

Notes and reminders

DAYS SOBER OR NUMBER OF DAYS SINCE ENGAGING IN A HARMFUL OR DESTRUCTIVE BEHAVIOR

BEHAVIOR	DAYS SINCE

THURSDAY

Skills practiced

MINDFULNESS	EMOTION REGULATION	DISTRESS TOLERANCE	INTERPERSONAL EFFECTIVENESS

Things that I'm **thankful** for

1.
2.
3.

Goals I worked towards

Today's **shining moment**

Notes and reminders

DAYS SOBER OR NUMBER OF DAYS SINCE ENGAGING IN A HARMFUL OR DESTRUCTIVE BEHAVIOR

BEHAVIOR	DAYS SINCE

FRIDAY

Skills practiced

MINDFULNESS	EMOTION REGULATION	DISTRESS TOLERANCE	INTERPERSONAL EFFECTIVENESS

Things that I'm **thankful** for

1.
2.
3.

Goals I worked towards

Today's **shining moment**

Notes and reminders

DAYS SOBER OR NUMBER OF DAYS SINCE ENGAGING IN A HARMFUL OR DESTRUCTIVE BEHAVIOR

BEHAVIOR	DAYS SINCE

SATURDAY

DATE / /

Skills practiced

MINDFULNESS	EMOTION REGULATION	DISTRESS TOLERANCE	INTERPERSONAL EFFECTIVENESS

Things that I'm **thankful** for

1.
2.
3.

Goals I worked towards

Today's **shining moment**

Notes and reminders

DAYS SOBER OR NUMBER OF DAYS SINCE ENGAGING IN A HARMFUL OR DESTRUCTIVE BEHAVIOR

BEHAVIOR	DAYS SINCE

SUNDAY

DATE / /

Skills practiced

MINDFULNESS	EMOTION REGULATION	DISTRESS TOLERANCE	INTERPERSONAL EFFECTIVENESS

Things that I'm **thankful** for

1.
2.
3.

Goals I worked towards

Today's **shining moment**

Notes and reminders

DAYS SOBER OR NUMBER OF DAYS SINCE ENGAGING IN A HARMFUL OR DESTRUCTIVE BEHAVIOR

BEHAVIOR	DAYS SINCE

THE WEEK AHEAD

Daily self-care tracker

		M	T	W	T	F	S	S
PHYSICAL	Exercised for at least 10–15 minutes	✓						
	Took prescribed medications as directed	✗						
	Refrained from self-medicating							
	Got enough sleep							
	Ate balanced meals							
EMOTIONAL	Skillfully tolerated distressing moments							
	Validated my own thoughts, emotions, and experiences							
	Practiced self-compassion							
	Engaged in mindful breathing or breath counting							
	Observed and described feelings mindfully							
RELATIONAL	Practiced empathy and unconditional kindness							
	Let go of judgments about others							
	Used problem-solving skills to strengthen relationships							
	Said no and established limits when necessary							
	Expressed a mindful interest in others							
SPIRITUAL	Used prayer or meditation to help myself							
	Sought or created meaning in my life							
	Allowed myself to be inspired or to inspire others							
	Honored my values and beliefs							
	Attended religious or spiritual services							

MONDAY

DATE   /   /

Skills practiced

MINDFULNESS	EMOTION REGULATION	DISTRESS TOLERANCE	INTERPERSONAL EFFECTIVENESS

Things that I'm **thankful** for

1.
2.
3.

Goals I worked towards

Today's **shining moment**

Notes and reminders

DAYS SOBER
OR NUMBER OF DAYS SINCE ENGAGING IN A HARMFUL OR DESTRUCTIVE BEHAVIOR

BEHAVIOR	DAYS SINCE

TUESDAY

Skills practiced

MINDFULNESS	EMOTION REGULATION	DISTRESS TOLERANCE	INTERPERSONAL EFFECTIVENESS

Things that I'm **thankful** for

1.
2.
3.

Goals I worked towards

Today's **shining moment**

Notes and reminders

DAYS SOBER
OR NUMBER OF DAYS SINCE ENGAGING IN A HARMFUL OR DESTRUCTIVE BEHAVIOR

BEHAVIOR	DAYS SINCE

WEDNESDAY

Skills practiced

MINDFULNESS	EMOTION REGULATION	DISTRESS TOLERANCE	INTERPERSONAL EFFECTIVENESS

Things that I'm **thankful** for

1.
2.
3.

Goals I worked towards

Today's **shining moment**

Notes and reminders

DAYS SOBER
OR NUMBER OF DAYS SINCE ENGAGING IN A HARMFUL OR DESTRUCTIVE BEHAVIOR

BEHAVIOR	DAYS SINCE

THURSDAY

DATE   /   /

Skills practiced

MINDFULNESS	EMOTION REGULATION	DISTRESS TOLERANCE	INTERPERSONAL EFFECTIVENESS

Things that I'm **thankful** for

1.
2.
3.

Goals I worked towards

Today's **shining moment**

Notes and reminders

DAYS SOBER OR NUMBER OF DAYS SINCE ENGAGING IN A HARMFUL OR DESTRUCTIVE BEHAVIOR

BEHAVIOR	DAYS SINCE

FRIDAY

DATE   /   /

Skills practiced

MINDFULNESS	EMOTION REGULATION	DISTRESS TOLERANCE	INTERPERSONAL EFFECTIVENESS

Things that I'm **thankful** for

1.
2.
3.

Goals I worked towards

Today's **shining moment**

Notes and reminders

DAYS SOBER OR NUMBER OF DAYS SINCE ENGAGING IN A HARMFUL OR DESTRUCTIVE BEHAVIOR

BEHAVIOR	DAYS SINCE

SATURDAY

DATE   /   /

Skills practiced

MINDFULNESS	EMOTION REGULATION	DISTRESS TOLERANCE	INTERPERSONAL EFFECTIVENESS

Things that I'm **thankful** for

1.
2.
3.

Goals I worked towards

Today's **shining moment**

Notes and reminders

DAYS SOBER
OR NUMBER OF DAYS SINCE ENGAGING IN A HARMFUL OR DESTRUCTIVE BEHAVIOR

BEHAVIOR	DAYS SINCE

SUNDAY

DATE   /   /

Skills practiced

MINDFULNESS	EMOTION REGULATION	DISTRESS TOLERANCE	INTERPERSONAL EFFECTIVENESS

Things that I'm **thankful** for

1.
2.
3.

Goals I worked towards

Today's **shining moment**

Notes and reminders

DAYS SOBER
OR NUMBER OF DAYS SINCE ENGAGING IN A HARMFUL OR DESTRUCTIVE BEHAVIOR

BEHAVIOR	DAYS SINCE

SELF-CARE ASSESSMENT

Over the past 28 days, how often have you engaged in these specific self-care methods?

PHYSICAL CARE	SCORE
Ate small balanced meals throughout the day	
Exercised for at least 15–20 minutes each day	
Followed preventive care instructions	
Bathed and brushed teeth daily	
Balanced sleep	
Refrained from self-medicating with alcohol, drugs, or prescription medicine	
Treated illness promptly	

TOTAL SCORE FOR THIS SECTION

EMOTIONAL CARE	SCORE
Attended all scheduled treatment and therapy appointments	
Made time for hobbies and enjoyable activities	
Politely said no to unwanted requests	
Let others know when I needed extra help	
Spent time with friends and loved ones	
Validated my own emotions, thoughts, and experiences	
Practiced self-compassion	

TOTAL SCORE FOR THIS SECTION

TOTAL SCORE PER SECTION

20-28	**Excellent!** You're doing a great job of taking care of yourself in this area.
11-19	**Very good.** Identify and address any gaps in self-care.
Below 10	**No one is perfect.** Is this an area of growth for you?

Remember, a score of zero (not applicable) in any area may lower your section score.

RELATIONAL CARE	SCORE
Stayed connected to friends and family members	
Set aside time to spend with people I care about	
Told people close to me that they were important	
Apologized or made repairs when I was wrong	
Expressed appreciation and thankfulness to others	
Empathized with others or thought about problems from their perspective	
Established limits and boundaries when necessary	

TOTAL SCORE FOR THIS SECTION

SPIRITUAL CARE	SCORE
Attended religious or spiritual services	
Spent time with others who share similar beliefs	
Sought spiritual direction or guidance	
Prayed or asked someone to pray for me	
Practiced mindfulness and/or meditation	
Identified important values and sought meaning in my life	
Read or watched things that helped to inspire me	

TOTAL SCORE FOR THIS SECTION

THE WEEK AHEAD

Daily self-care tracker

		M	T	W	T	F	S	S
PHYSICAL	Exercised for at least 10-15 minutes	✓/✗						
	Took prescribed medications as directed							
	Refrained from self-medicating							
	Got enough sleep							
	Ate balanced meals							
EMOTIONAL	Skillfully tolerated distressing moments							
	Validated my own thoughts, emotions, and experiences							
	Practiced self-compassion							
	Engaged in mindful breathing or breath counting							
	Observed and described feelings mindfully							
RELATIONAL	Practiced empathy and unconditional kindness							
	Let go of judgments about others							
	Used problem-solving skills to strengthen relationships							
	Said no and established limits when necessary							
	Expressed a mindful interest in others							
SPIRITUAL	Used prayer or meditation to help myself							
	Sought or created meaning in my life							
	Allowed myself to be inspired or to inspire others							
	Honored my values and beliefs							
	Attended religious or spiritual services							

MONDAY

DATE / /

Skills practiced

MINDFULNESS	EMOTION REGULATION	DISTRESS TOLERANCE	INTERPERSONAL EFFECTIVENESS

Things that I'm **thankful** for

1.
2.
3.

Goals I worked towards

Today's **shining moment**

Notes and reminders

DAYS SOBER
OR NUMBER OF DAYS SINCE ENGAGING IN A HARMFUL OR DESTRUCTIVE BEHAVIOR

BEHAVIOR	DAYS SINCE

TUESDAY

Skills practiced

MINDFULNESS	EMOTION REGULATION	DISTRESS TOLERANCE	INTERPERSONAL EFFECTIVENESS

Things that I'm **thankful** for

1.
2.
3.

Goals I worked towards

Today's **shining moment**

Notes and reminders

DAYS SOBER
OR NUMBER OF DAYS SINCE ENGAGING IN A HARMFUL OR DESTRUCTIVE BEHAVIOR

BEHAVIOR	DAYS SINCE

WEDNESDAY

Skills practiced

MINDFULNESS	EMOTION REGULATION	DISTRESS TOLERANCE	INTERPERSONAL EFFECTIVENESS

Things that I'm **thankful** for

1.
2.
3.

Goals I worked towards

Today's **shining moment**

Notes and reminders

DAYS SOBER
OR NUMBER OF DAYS SINCE ENGAGING IN A HARMFUL OR DESTRUCTIVE BEHAVIOR

BEHAVIOR	DAYS SINCE

THURSDAY

DATE   /   /

Skills practiced

MINDFULNESS	EMOTION REGULATION	DISTRESS TOLERANCE	INTERPERSONAL EFFECTIVENESS

Things that I'm **thankful** for

1.
2.
3.

Goals I worked towards

Today's **shining moment**

Notes and reminders

DAYS SOBER
OR NUMBER OF DAYS SINCE ENGAGING IN A HARMFUL OR DESTRUCTIVE BEHAVIOR

BEHAVIOR	DAYS SINCE

FRIDAY

DATE   /   /

Skills practiced

MINDFULNESS	EMOTION REGULATION	DISTRESS TOLERANCE	INTERPERSONAL EFFECTIVENESS

Things that I'm **thankful** for

1.
2.
3.

Goals I worked towards

Today's **shining moment**

Notes and reminders

DAYS SOBER
OR NUMBER OF DAYS SINCE ENGAGING IN A HARMFUL OR DESTRUCTIVE BEHAVIOR

BEHAVIOR	DAYS SINCE

SATURDAY

DATE / /

Skills practiced

MINDFULNESS	EMOTION REGULATION	DISTRESS TOLERANCE	INTERPERSONAL EFFECTIVENESS

Things that I'm **thankful** for

1.
2.
3.

Goals I worked towards

Today's **shining moment**

Notes and reminders

DAYS SOBER
OR NUMBER OF DAYS SINCE ENGAGING IN A HARMFUL OR DESTRUCTIVE BEHAVIOR

BEHAVIOR	DAYS SINCE

SUNDAY

DATE / /

Skills practiced

MINDFULNESS	EMOTION REGULATION	DISTRESS TOLERANCE	INTERPERSONAL EFFECTIVENESS

Things that I'm **thankful** for

1.
2.
3.

Goals I worked towards

Today's **shining moment**

Notes and reminders

DAYS SOBER
OR NUMBER OF DAYS SINCE ENGAGING IN A HARMFUL OR DESTRUCTIVE BEHAVIOR

BEHAVIOR	DAYS SINCE

THE WEEK AHEAD

Daily self-care tracker

		M	T	W	T	F	S	S
PHYSICAL	Exercised for at least 10–15 minutes	✓						
	Took prescribed medications as directed	✗						
	Refrained from self-medicating							
	Got enough sleep							
	Ate balanced meals							
EMOTIONAL	Skillfully tolerated distressing moments							
	Validated my own thoughts, emotions, and experiences							
	Practiced self-compassion							
	Engaged in mindful breathing or breath counting							
	Observed and described feelings mindfully							
RELATIONAL	Practiced empathy and unconditional kindness							
	Let go of judgments about others							
	Used problem-solving skills to strengthen relationships							
	Said no and established limits when necessary							
	Expressed a mindful interest in others							
SPIRITUAL	Used prayer or meditation to help myself							
	Sought or created meaning in my life							
	Allowed myself to be inspired or to inspire others							
	Honored my values and beliefs							
	Attended religious or spiritual services							

MONDAY

DATE   /   /

Skills practiced

MINDFULNESS	EMOTION REGULATION	DISTRESS TOLERANCE	INTERPERSONAL EFFECTIVENESS

Things that I'm **thankful** for

1.
2.
3.

Goals I worked towards

Today's **shining moment**

Notes and reminders

DAYS SOBER
OR NUMBER OF DAYS SINCE ENGAGING IN A HARMFUL OR DESTRUCTIVE BEHAVIOR

BEHAVIOR	DAYS SINCE

TUESDAY

DATE / /

Skills practiced

MINDFULNESS	EMOTION REGULATION	DISTRESS TOLERANCE	INTERPERSONAL EFFECTIVENESS

Things that I'm **thankful** for

1.
2.
3.

Goals I worked towards

Today's **shining moment**

Notes and reminders

DAYS SOBER OR NUMBER OF DAYS SINCE ENGAGING IN A HARMFUL OR DESTRUCTIVE BEHAVIOR

BEHAVIOR	DAYS SINCE

WEDNESDAY

DATE / /

Skills practiced

MINDFULNESS	EMOTION REGULATION	DISTRESS TOLERANCE	INTERPERSONAL EFFECTIVENESS

Things that I'm **thankful** for

1.
2.
3.

Goals I worked towards

Today's **shining moment**

Notes and reminders

DAYS SOBER OR NUMBER OF DAYS SINCE ENGAGING IN A HARMFUL OR DESTRUCTIVE BEHAVIOR

BEHAVIOR	DAYS SINCE

THURSDAY

DATE / /

Skills practiced

MINDFULNESS	EMOTION REGULATION	DISTRESS TOLERANCE	INTERPERSONAL EFFECTIVENESS

Things that I'm **thankful** for

1.
2.
3.

Goals I worked towards

Today's **shining moment**

Notes and reminders

DAYS SOBER OR NUMBER OF DAYS SINCE ENGAGING IN A HARMFUL OR DESTRUCTIVE BEHAVIOR

BEHAVIOR	DAYS SINCE

FRIDAY

DATE / /

Skills practiced

MINDFULNESS	EMOTION REGULATION	DISTRESS TOLERANCE	INTERPERSONAL EFFECTIVENESS

Things that I'm **thankful** for

1.
2.
3.

Goals I worked towards

Today's **shining moment**

Notes and reminders

DAYS SOBER OR NUMBER OF DAYS SINCE ENGAGING IN A HARMFUL OR DESTRUCTIVE BEHAVIOR

BEHAVIOR	DAYS SINCE

SATURDAY

DATE   /   /

Skills practiced

MINDFULNESS	EMOTION REGULATION	DISTRESS TOLERANCE	INTERPERSONAL EFFECTIVENESS

Things that I'm **thankful** for

1.
2.
3.

Goals I worked towards

Today's **shining moment**

Notes and reminders

DAYS SOBER OR NUMBER OF DAYS SINCE ENGAGING IN A HARMFUL OR DESTRUCTIVE BEHAVIOR

BEHAVIOR	DAYS SINCE

SUNDAY

DATE   /   /

Skills practiced

MINDFULNESS	EMOTION REGULATION	DISTRESS TOLERANCE	INTERPERSONAL EFFECTIVENESS

Things that I'm **thankful** for

1.
2.
3.

Goals I worked towards

Today's **shining moment**

Notes and reminders

DAYS SOBER OR NUMBER OF DAYS SINCE ENGAGING IN A HARMFUL OR DESTRUCTIVE BEHAVIOR

BEHAVIOR	DAYS SINCE

THE WEEK AHEAD

Daily self-care tracker

		M	T	W	T	F	S	S
PHYSICAL	Exercised for at least 10–15 minutes							
	Took prescribed medications as directed							
	Refrained from self-medicating							
	Got enough sleep							
	Ate balanced meals							
EMOTIONAL	Skillfully tolerated distressing moments							
	Validated my own thoughts, emotions, and experiences							
	Practiced self-compassion							
	Engaged in mindful breathing or breath counting							
	Observed and described feelings mindfully							
RELATIONAL	Practiced empathy and unconditional kindness							
	Let go of judgments about others							
	Used problem-solving skills to strengthen relationships							
	Said no and established limits when necessary							
	Expressed a mindful interest in others							
SPIRITUAL	Used prayer or meditation to help myself							
	Sought or created meaning in my life							
	Allowed myself to be inspired or to inspire others							
	Honored my values and beliefs							
	Attended religious or spiritual services							

MONDAY

DATE   /   /

Skills practiced

MINDFULNESS	EMOTION REGULATION	DISTRESS TOLERANCE	INTERPERSONAL EFFECTIVENESS

Things that I'm **thankful** for

1.
2.
3.

Goals I worked towards

Today's **shining moment**

Notes and reminders

DAYS SOBER OR NUMBER OF DAYS SINCE ENGAGING IN A HARMFUL OR DESTRUCTIVE BEHAVIOR

BEHAVIOR	DAYS SINCE

TUESDAY

Skills practiced

MINDFULNESS	EMOTION REGULATION	DISTRESS TOLERANCE	INTERPERSONAL EFFECTIVENESS

Things that I'm **thankful** for

1.
2.
3.

Goals I worked towards

Today's **shining moment**

Notes and reminders

DAYS SOBER OR NUMBER OF DAYS SINCE ENGAGING IN A HARMFUL OR DESTRUCTIVE BEHAVIOR

BEHAVIOR	DAYS SINCE

WEDNESDAY

DATE / /

Skills practiced

MINDFULNESS	EMOTION REGULATION	DISTRESS TOLERANCE	INTERPERSONAL EFFECTIVENESS

Things that I'm **thankful** for

1.
2.
3.

Goals I worked towards

Today's **shining moment**

Notes and reminders

DAYS SOBER OR NUMBER OF DAYS SINCE ENGAGING IN A HARMFUL OR DESTRUCTIVE BEHAVIOR

BEHAVIOR	DAYS SINCE

THURSDAY

Skills practiced

MINDFULNESS	EMOTION REGULATION	DISTRESS TOLERANCE	INTERPERSONAL EFFECTIVENESS

Things that I'm **thankful** for

1.
2.
3.

Goals I worked towards

Today's **shining moment**

Notes and reminders

DAYS SOBER OR NUMBER OF DAYS SINCE ENGAGING IN A HARMFUL OR DESTRUCTIVE BEHAVIOR

BEHAVIOR	DAYS SINCE

FRIDAY

Skills practiced

MINDFULNESS	EMOTION REGULATION	DISTRESS TOLERANCE	INTERPERSONAL EFFECTIVENESS

Things that I'm **thankful** for

1.
2.
3.

Goals I worked towards

Today's **shining moment**

Notes and reminders

DAYS SOBER OR NUMBER OF DAYS SINCE ENGAGING IN A HARMFUL OR DESTRUCTIVE BEHAVIOR

BEHAVIOR	DAYS SINCE

SATURDAY

Skills practiced

MINDFULNESS	EMOTION REGULATION	DISTRESS TOLERANCE	INTERPERSONAL EFFECTIVENESS

Things that I'm **thankful** for

1.
2.
3.

Goals I worked towards

Today's **shining moment**

Notes and reminders

DAYS SOBER
OR NUMBER OF DAYS SINCE ENGAGING IN A HARMFUL OR DESTRUCTIVE BEHAVIOR

BEHAVIOR	DAYS SINCE

SUNDAY

DATE   /   /

Skills practiced

MINDFULNESS	EMOTION REGULATION	DISTRESS TOLERANCE	INTERPERSONAL EFFECTIVENESS

Things that I'm **thankful** for

1.
2.
3.

Goals I worked towards

Today's **shining moment**

Notes and reminders

DAYS SOBER
OR NUMBER OF DAYS SINCE ENGAGING IN A HARMFUL OR DESTRUCTIVE BEHAVIOR

BEHAVIOR	DAYS SINCE

THE WEEK AHEAD

Daily self-care tracker

		M	T	W	T	F	S	S
PHYSICAL	Exercised for at least 10-15 minutes	✓/✗						
	Took prescribed medications as directed							
	Refrained from self-medicating							
	Got enough sleep							
	Ate balanced meals							
EMOTIONAL	Skillfully tolerated distressing moments							
	Validated my own thoughts, emotions, and experiences							
	Practiced self-compassion							
	Engaged in mindful breathing or breath counting							
	Observed and described feelings mindfully							
RELATIONAL	Practiced empathy and unconditional kindness							
	Let go of judgments about others							
	Used problem-solving skills to strengthen relationships							
	Said no and established limits when necessary							
	Expressed a mindful interest in others							
SPIRITUAL	Used prayer or meditation to help myself							
	Sought or created meaning in my life							
	Allowed myself to be inspired or to inspire others							
	Honored my values and beliefs							
	Attended religious or spiritual services							

MONDAY

DATE / /

Skills practiced

MINDFULNESS	EMOTION REGULATION	DISTRESS TOLERANCE	INTERPERSONAL EFFECTIVENESS

Things that I'm **thankful** for

1.
2.
3.

Goals I worked towards

Today's **shining moment**

Notes and reminders

DAYS SOBER
OR NUMBER OF DAYS SINCE ENGAGING IN A HARMFUL OR DESTRUCTIVE BEHAVIOR

BEHAVIOR	DAYS SINCE

TUESDAY

DATE   /   /

Skills practiced

MINDFULNESS	EMOTION REGULATION	DISTRESS TOLERANCE	INTERPERSONAL EFFECTIVENESS

Things that I'm **thankful** for

1.
2.
3.

Goals I worked towards

Today's **shining moment**

Notes and reminders

DAYS SOBER
OR NUMBER OF DAYS SINCE ENGAGING IN A HARMFUL OR DESTRUCTIVE BEHAVIOR

BEHAVIOR	DAYS SINCE

WEDNESDAY

DATE   /   /

Skills practiced

MINDFULNESS	EMOTION REGULATION	DISTRESS TOLERANCE	INTERPERSONAL EFFECTIVENESS

Things that I'm **thankful** for

1.
2.
3.

Goals I worked towards

Today's **shining moment**

Notes and reminders

DAYS SOBER
OR NUMBER OF DAYS SINCE ENGAGING IN A HARMFUL OR DESTRUCTIVE BEHAVIOR

BEHAVIOR	DAYS SINCE

THURSDAY

DATE   /   /

Skills practiced

MINDFULNESS	EMOTION REGULATION	DISTRESS TOLERANCE	INTERPERSONAL EFFECTIVENESS

Things that I'm **thankful** for

1.

2.

3.

Goals I worked towards

Today's **shining moment**

Notes and reminders

DAYS SOBER OR NUMBER OF DAYS SINCE ENGAGING IN A HARMFUL OR DESTRUCTIVE BEHAVIOR

BEHAVIOR	DAYS SINCE

FRIDAY

DATE   /   /

Skills practiced

MINDFULNESS	EMOTION REGULATION	DISTRESS TOLERANCE	INTERPERSONAL EFFECTIVENESS

Things that I'm **thankful** for

1.

2.

3.

Goals I worked towards

Today's **shining moment**

Notes and reminders

DAYS SOBER OR NUMBER OF DAYS SINCE ENGAGING IN A HARMFUL OR DESTRUCTIVE BEHAVIOR

BEHAVIOR	DAYS SINCE

SATURDAY

DATE   /   /

Skills practiced

MINDFULNESS	EMOTION REGULATION	DISTRESS TOLERANCE	INTERPERSONAL EFFECTIVENESS

Things that I'm **thankful** for

1.
2.
3.

Goals I worked towards

Today's **shining moment**

Notes and reminders

DAYS SOBER OR NUMBER OF DAYS SINCE ENGAGING IN A HARMFUL OR DESTRUCTIVE BEHAVIOR

BEHAVIOR	DAYS SINCE

SUNDAY

DATE   /   /

Skills practiced

MINDFULNESS	EMOTION REGULATION	DISTRESS TOLERANCE	INTERPERSONAL EFFECTIVENESS

Things that I'm **thankful** for

1.
2.
3.

Goals I worked towards

Today's **shining moment**

Notes and reminders

DAYS SOBER OR NUMBER OF DAYS SINCE ENGAGING IN A HARMFUL OR DESTRUCTIVE BEHAVIOR

BEHAVIOR	DAYS SINCE

SELF-CARE ASSESSMENT

Over the past 28 days, how often have you engaged in these specific self-care methods?

SCORING

4 **Always**

3 **Often**

2 **Sometimes**

1 **Rarely**

0 Not applicable to me at this time

PHYSICAL CARE	SCORE
Ate small balanced meals throughout the day	
Exercised for at least 15-20 minutes each day	
Followed preventive care instructions	
Bathed and brushed teeth daily	
Balanced sleep	
Refrained from self-medicating with alcohol, drugs, or prescription medicine	
Treated illness promptly	

TOTAL SCORE FOR THIS SECTION

EMOTIONAL CARE	SCORE
Attended all scheduled treatment and therapy appointments	
Made time for hobbies and enjoyable activities	
Politely said no to unwanted requests	
Let others know when I needed extra help	
Spent time with friends and loved ones	
Validated my own emotions, thoughts, and experiences	
Practiced self-compassion	

TOTAL SCORE FOR THIS SECTION

TOTAL SCORE PER SECTION

20-28	**Excellent!** You're doing a great job of taking care of yourself in this area.
11-19	**Very good.** Identify and address any gaps in self-care.
Below 10	**No one is perfect.** Is this an area of growth for you?

Remember, a score of zero (not applicable) in any area may lower your section score.

RELATIONAL CARE	SCORE
Stayed connected to friends and family members	
Set aside time to spend with people I care about	
Told people close to me that they were important	
Apologized or made repairs when I was wrong	
Expressed appreciation and thankfulness to others	
Empathized with others or thought about problems from their perspective	
Established limits and boundaries when necessary	

TOTAL SCORE FOR THIS SECTION

SPIRITUAL CARE	SCORE
Attended religious or spiritual services	
Spent time with others who share similar beliefs	
Sought spiritual direction or guidance	
Prayed or asked someone to pray for me	
Practiced mindfulness and/or meditation	
Identified important values and sought meaning in my life	
Read or watched things that helped to inspire me	

TOTAL SCORE FOR THIS SECTION

THE WEEK AHEAD

Daily self-care tracker

		M	T	W	T	F	S	S
PHYSICAL	Exercised for at least 10-15 minutes	✓						
	Took prescribed medications as directed	✗						
	Refrained from self-medicating							
	Got enough sleep							
	Ate balanced meals							
EMOTIONAL	Skillfully tolerated distressing moments							
	Validated my own thoughts, emotions, and experiences							
	Practiced self-compassion							
	Engaged in mindful breathing or breath counting							
	Observed and described feelings mindfully							
RELATIONAL	Practiced empathy and unconditional kindness							
	Let go of judgments about others							
	Used problem-solving skills to strengthen relationships							
	Said no and established limits when necessary							
	Expressed a mindful interest in others							
SPIRITUAL	Used prayer or meditation to help myself							
	Sought or created meaning in my life							
	Allowed myself to be inspired or to inspire others							
	Honored my values and beliefs							
	Attended religious or spiritual services							

MONDAY

DATE   /   /

Skills practiced

MINDFULNESS	EMOTION REGULATION	DISTRESS TOLERANCE	INTERPERSONAL EFFECTIVENESS

Things that I'm **thankful** for

1.

2.

3.

Goals I worked towards

Today's **shining moment**

Notes and reminders

DAYS SOBER
OR NUMBER OF DAYS SINCE ENGAGING IN A HARMFUL OR DESTRUCTIVE BEHAVIOR

BEHAVIOR	DAYS SINCE

TUESDAY

DATE   /   /

Skills practiced

MINDFULNESS	EMOTION REGULATION	DISTRESS TOLERANCE	INTERPERSONAL EFFECTIVENESS

Things that I'm **thankful** for

1.
2.
3.

Goals I worked towards

Today's **shining moment**

Notes and reminders

DAYS SOBER
OR NUMBER OF DAYS SINCE ENGAGING IN A HARMFUL OR DESTRUCTIVE BEHAVIOR

BEHAVIOR	DAYS SINCE

WEDNESDAY

DATE   /   /

Skills practiced

MINDFULNESS	EMOTION REGULATION	DISTRESS TOLERANCE	INTERPERSONAL EFFECTIVENESS

Things that I'm **thankful** for

1.
2.
3.

Goals I worked towards

Today's **shining moment**

Notes and reminders

DAYS SOBER
OR NUMBER OF DAYS SINCE ENGAGING IN A HARMFUL OR DESTRUCTIVE BEHAVIOR

BEHAVIOR	DAYS SINCE

THURSDAY

Skills practiced

MINDFULNESS	EMOTION REGULATION	DISTRESS TOLERANCE	INTERPERSONAL EFFECTIVENESS

Things that I'm **thankful** for

1.
2.
3.

Goals I worked towards

Today's **shining moment**

Notes and reminders

DAYS SOBER
OR NUMBER OF DAYS SINCE ENGAGING IN A HARMFUL OR DESTRUCTIVE BEHAVIOR

BEHAVIOR	DAYS SINCE

FRIDAY

Skills practiced

MINDFULNESS	EMOTION REGULATION	DISTRESS TOLERANCE	INTERPERSONAL EFFECTIVENESS

Things that I'm **thankful** for

1.
2.
3.

Goals I worked towards

Today's **shining moment**

Notes and reminders

DAYS SOBER
OR NUMBER OF DAYS SINCE ENGAGING IN A HARMFUL OR DESTRUCTIVE BEHAVIOR

BEHAVIOR	DAYS SINCE

SATURDAY

DATE / /

Skills practiced

MINDFULNESS	EMOTION REGULATION	DISTRESS TOLERANCE	INTERPERSONAL EFFECTIVENESS

Things that I'm **thankful** for

1.
2.
3.

Goals I worked towards

Today's **shining moment**

Notes and reminders

DAYS SOBER
OR NUMBER OF DAYS SINCE ENGAGING IN A HARMFUL OR DESTRUCTIVE BEHAVIOR

BEHAVIOR	DAYS SINCE

SUNDAY

DATE / /

Skills practiced

MINDFULNESS	EMOTION REGULATION	DISTRESS TOLERANCE	INTERPERSONAL EFFECTIVENESS

Things that I'm **thankful** for

1.
2.
3.

Goals I worked towards

Today's **shining moment**

Notes and reminders

DAYS SOBER
OR NUMBER OF DAYS SINCE ENGAGING IN A HARMFUL OR DESTRUCTIVE BEHAVIOR

BEHAVIOR	DAYS SINCE

THE WEEK AHEAD

Daily self-care tracker

		M	T	W	T	F	S	S
PHYSICAL	Exercised for at least 10–15 minutes	✓/✗						
	Took prescribed medications as directed							
	Refrained from self-medicating							
	Got enough sleep							
	Ate balanced meals							
EMOTIONAL	Skillfully tolerated distressing moments							
	Validated my own thoughts, emotions, and experiences							
	Practiced self-compassion							
	Engaged in mindful breathing or breath counting							
	Observed and described feelings mindfully							
RELATIONAL	Practiced empathy and unconditional kindness							
	Let go of judgments about others							
	Used problem-solving skills to strengthen relationships							
	Said no and established limits when necessary							
	Expressed a mindful interest in others							
SPIRITUAL	Used prayer or meditation to help myself							
	Sought or created meaning in my life							
	Allowed myself to be inspired or to inspire others							
	Honored my values and beliefs							
	Attended religious or spiritual services							

MONDAY

DATE   /   /

Skills practiced

MINDFULNESS	EMOTION REGULATION	DISTRESS TOLERANCE	INTERPERSONAL EFFECTIVENESS

Things that I'm **thankful** for

1.
2.
3.

Goals I worked towards

Today's **shining moment**

Notes and reminders

DAYS SOBER
OR NUMBER OF DAYS SINCE ENGAGING IN A HARMFUL OR DESTRUCTIVE BEHAVIOR

BEHAVIOR	DAYS SINCE
	☐ ☐ ☐
	☐ ☐ ☐
	☐ ☐ ☐

TUESDAY

Skills practiced

MINDFULNESS	EMOTION REGULATION	DISTRESS TOLERANCE	INTERPERSONAL EFFECTIVENESS

Things that I'm **thankful** for

1.
2.
3.

Goals I worked towards

Today's **shining moment**

Notes and reminders

DAYS SOBER OR NUMBER OF DAYS SINCE ENGAGING IN A HARMFUL OR DESTRUCTIVE BEHAVIOR

BEHAVIOR	DAYS SINCE

WEDNESDAY

Skills practiced

MINDFULNESS	EMOTION REGULATION	DISTRESS TOLERANCE	INTERPERSONAL EFFECTIVENESS

Things that I'm **thankful** for

1.
2.
3.

Goals I worked towards

Today's **shining moment**

Notes and reminders

DAYS SOBER OR NUMBER OF DAYS SINCE ENGAGING IN A HARMFUL OR DESTRUCTIVE BEHAVIOR

BEHAVIOR	DAYS SINCE

THURSDAY

DATE / /

Skills practiced

MINDFULNESS	EMOTION REGULATION	DISTRESS TOLERANCE	INTERPERSONAL EFFECTIVENESS

Things that I'm **thankful** for

1.
2.
3.

Goals I worked towards

Today's **shining moment**

Notes and reminders

DAYS SOBER
OR NUMBER OF DAYS SINCE ENGAGING IN A HARMFUL OR DESTRUCTIVE BEHAVIOR

BEHAVIOR	DAYS SINCE

FRIDAY

DATE / /

Skills practiced

MINDFULNESS	EMOTION REGULATION	DISTRESS TOLERANCE	INTERPERSONAL EFFECTIVENESS

Things that I'm **thankful** for

1.
2.
3.

Goals I worked towards

Today's **shining moment**

Notes and reminders

DAYS SOBER
OR NUMBER OF DAYS SINCE ENGAGING IN A HARMFUL OR DESTRUCTIVE BEHAVIOR

BEHAVIOR	DAYS SINCE

SATURDAY

DATE / /

Skills practiced

MINDFULNESS	EMOTION REGULATION	DISTRESS TOLERANCE	INTERPERSONAL EFFECTIVENESS

Things that I'm **thankful** for

1.
2.
3.

Goals I worked towards

Today's **shining moment**

Notes and reminders

DAYS SOBER
OR NUMBER OF DAYS SINCE ENGAGING IN A HARMFUL OR DESTRUCTIVE BEHAVIOR

BEHAVIOR	DAYS SINCE

SUNDAY

DATE / /

Skills practiced

MINDFULNESS	EMOTION REGULATION	DISTRESS TOLERANCE	INTERPERSONAL EFFECTIVENESS

Things that I'm **thankful** for

1.
2.
3.

Goals I worked towards

Today's **shining moment**

Notes and reminders

DAYS SOBER
OR NUMBER OF DAYS SINCE ENGAGING IN A HARMFUL OR DESTRUCTIVE BEHAVIOR

BEHAVIOR	DAYS SINCE

THE WEEK AHEAD

Daily self-care tracker

		M	T	W	T	F	S	S
PHYSICAL	Exercised for at least 10–15 minutes							
	Took prescribed medications as directed							
	Refrained from self-medicating							
	Got enough sleep							
	Ate balanced meals							
EMOTIONAL	Skillfully tolerated distressing moments							
	Validated my own thoughts, emotions, and experiences							
	Practiced self-compassion							
	Engaged in mindful breathing or breath counting							
	Observed and described feelings mindfully							
RELATIONAL	Practiced empathy and unconditional kindness							
	Let go of judgments about others							
	Used problem-solving skills to strengthen relationships							
	Said no and established limits when necessary							
	Expressed a mindful interest in others							
SPIRITUAL	Used prayer or meditation to help myself							
	Sought or created meaning in my life							
	Allowed myself to be inspired or to inspire others							
	Honored my values and beliefs							
	Attended religious or spiritual services							

MONDAY

DATE   /   /

Skills practiced

MINDFULNESS	EMOTION REGULATION	DISTRESS TOLERANCE	INTERPERSONAL EFFECTIVENESS

Things that I'm **thankful** for

1.
2.
3.

Goals I worked towards

Today's **shining moment**

Notes and reminders

DAYS SOBER OR NUMBER OF DAYS SINCE ENGAGING IN A HARMFUL OR DESTRUCTIVE BEHAVIOR

BEHAVIOR	DAYS SINCE

TUESDAY

Skills practiced

MINDFULNESS	EMOTION REGULATION	DISTRESS TOLERANCE	INTERPERSONAL EFFECTIVENESS

Things that I'm **thankful** for

1.
2.
3.

Goals I worked towards

Today's **shining moment**

Notes and reminders

DAYS SOBER
OR NUMBER OF DAYS SINCE ENGAGING IN A HARMFUL OR DESTRUCTIVE BEHAVIOR

BEHAVIOR	DAYS SINCE

WEDNESDAY

DATE / /

Skills practiced

MINDFULNESS	EMOTION REGULATION	DISTRESS TOLERANCE	INTERPERSONAL EFFECTIVENESS

Things that I'm **thankful** for

1.
2.
3.

Goals I worked towards

Today's **shining moment**

Notes and reminders

DAYS SOBER
OR NUMBER OF DAYS SINCE ENGAGING IN A HARMFUL OR DESTRUCTIVE BEHAVIOR

BEHAVIOR	DAYS SINCE

THURSDAY

Skills practiced

MINDFULNESS	EMOTION REGULATION	DISTRESS TOLERANCE	INTERPERSONAL EFFECTIVENESS

Things that I'm **thankful** for

1.
2.
3.

Goals I worked towards

Today's **shining moment**

Notes and reminders

DAYS SOBER OR NUMBER OF DAYS SINCE ENGAGING IN A HARMFUL OR DESTRUCTIVE BEHAVIOR

BEHAVIOR	DAYS SINCE

FRIDAY

DATE   /   /

Skills practiced

MINDFULNESS	EMOTION REGULATION	DISTRESS TOLERANCE	INTERPERSONAL EFFECTIVENESS

Things that I'm **thankful** for

1.
2.
3.

Goals I worked towards

Today's **shining moment**

Notes and reminders

DAYS SOBER OR NUMBER OF DAYS SINCE ENGAGING IN A HARMFUL OR DESTRUCTIVE BEHAVIOR

BEHAVIOR	DAYS SINCE

SATURDAY

Skills practiced

MINDFULNESS	EMOTION REGULATION	DISTRESS TOLERANCE	INTERPERSONAL EFFECTIVENESS

Things that I'm thankful for

1.
2.
3.

Goals I worked towards

Today's shining moment

Notes and reminders

DAYS SOBER OR NUMBER OF DAYS SINCE ENGAGING IN A HARMFUL OR DESTRUCTIVE BEHAVIOR

BEHAVIOR	DAYS SINCE

SUNDAY

Skills practiced

MINDFULNESS	EMOTION REGULATION	DISTRESS TOLERANCE	INTERPERSONAL EFFECTIVENESS

Things that I'm thankful for

1.
2.
3.

Goals I worked towards

Today's shining moment

Notes and reminders

DAYS SOBER OR NUMBER OF DAYS SINCE ENGAGING IN A HARMFUL OR DESTRUCTIVE BEHAVIOR

BEHAVIOR	DAYS SINCE

THE WEEK AHEAD

Daily self-care tracker

		M	T	W	T	F	S	S
PHYSICAL	Exercised for at least 10-15 minutes	✓/✗						
	Took prescribed medications as directed							
	Refrained from self-medicating							
	Got enough sleep							
	Ate balanced meals							
EMOTIONAL	Skillfully tolerated distressing moments							
	Validated my own thoughts, emotions, and experiences							
	Practiced self-compassion							
	Engaged in mindful breathing or breath counting							
	Observed and described feelings mindfully							
RELATIONAL	Practiced empathy and unconditional kindness							
	Let go of judgments about others							
	Used problem-solving skills to strengthen relationships							
	Said no and established limits when necessary							
	Expressed a mindful interest in others							
SPIRITUAL	Used prayer or meditation to help myself							
	Sought or created meaning in my life							
	Allowed myself to be inspired or to inspire others							
	Honored my values and beliefs							
	Attended religious or spiritual services							

MONDAY

DATE   /   /

Skills practiced

MINDFULNESS	EMOTION REGULATION	DISTRESS TOLERANCE	INTERPERSONAL EFFECTIVENESS

Things that I'm **thankful** for

1.
2.
3.

Goals I worked towards

Today's **shining moment**

Notes and reminders

DAYS SOBER

OR NUMBER OF DAYS SINCE ENGAGING IN A HARMFUL OR DESTRUCTIVE BEHAVIOR

BEHAVIOR	DAYS SINCE

TUESDAY

Skills practiced

MINDFULNESS	EMOTION REGULATION	DISTRESS TOLERANCE	INTERPERSONAL EFFECTIVENESS

Things that I'm **thankful** for

1.
2.
3.

Goals I worked towards

Today's **shining moment**

Notes and reminders

DAYS SOBER OR NUMBER OF DAYS SINCE ENGAGING IN A HARMFUL OR DESTRUCTIVE BEHAVIOR	BEHAVIOR	DAYS SINCE

WEDNESDAY

Skills practiced

MINDFULNESS	EMOTION REGULATION	DISTRESS TOLERANCE	INTERPERSONAL EFFECTIVENESS

Things that I'm **thankful** for

1.
2.
3.

Goals I worked towards

Today's **shining moment**

Notes and reminders

DAYS SOBER OR NUMBER OF DAYS SINCE ENGAGING IN A HARMFUL OR DESTRUCTIVE BEHAVIOR	BEHAVIOR	DAYS SINCE

THURSDAY

DATE / /

Skills practiced

MINDFULNESS	EMOTION REGULATION	DISTRESS TOLERANCE	INTERPERSONAL EFFECTIVENESS

Things that I'm **thankful** for

1.
2.
3.

Goals I worked towards

Today's **shining moment**

Notes and reminders

DAYS SOBER
OR NUMBER OF DAYS SINCE ENGAGING IN A HARMFUL OR DESTRUCTIVE BEHAVIOR

BEHAVIOR	DAYS SINCE

FRIDAY

DATE / /

Skills practiced

MINDFULNESS	EMOTION REGULATION	DISTRESS TOLERANCE	INTERPERSONAL EFFECTIVENESS

Things that I'm **thankful** for

1.
2.
3.

Goals I worked towards

Today's **shining moment**

Notes and reminders

DAYS SOBER
OR NUMBER OF DAYS SINCE ENGAGING IN A HARMFUL OR DESTRUCTIVE BEHAVIOR

BEHAVIOR	DAYS SINCE

SATURDAY

Skills practiced

MINDFULNESS	EMOTION REGULATION	DISTRESS TOLERANCE	INTERPERSONAL EFFECTIVENESS

Things that I'm thankful for

1.
2.
3.

Goals I worked towards

Today's shining moment

Notes and reminders

DAYS SOBER
OR NUMBER OF DAYS SINCE ENGAGING IN A HARMFUL OR DESTRUCTIVE BEHAVIOR

BEHAVIOR	DAYS SINCE

SUNDAY

Skills practiced

MINDFULNESS	EMOTION REGULATION	DISTRESS TOLERANCE	INTERPERSONAL EFFECTIVENESS

Things that I'm thankful for

1.
2.
3.

Goals I worked towards

Today's shining moment

Notes and reminders

DAYS SOBER
OR NUMBER OF DAYS SINCE ENGAGING IN A HARMFUL OR DESTRUCTIVE BEHAVIOR

BEHAVIOR	DAYS SINCE

SELF-CARE ASSESSMENT

Over the past 28 days, how often have you engaged in these specific self-care methods?

PHYSICAL CARE	SCORE
Ate small balanced meals throughout the day	
Exercised for at least 15–20 minutes each day	
Followed preventive care instructions	
Bathed and brushed teeth daily	
Balanced sleep	
Refrained from self-medicating with alcohol, drugs, or prescription medicine	
Treated illness promptly	

TOTAL SCORE FOR THIS SECTION

EMOTIONAL CARE	SCORE
Attended all scheduled treatment and therapy appointments	
Made time for hobbies and enjoyable activities	
Politely said no to unwanted requests	
Let others know when I needed extra help	
Spent time with friends and loved ones	
Validated my own emotions, thoughts, and experiences	
Practiced self-compassion	

TOTAL SCORE FOR THIS SECTION

TOTAL SCORE PER SECTION

20-28	**Excellent!** You're doing a great job of taking care of yourself in this area.
11-19	**Very good.** Identify and address any gaps in self-care.
Below 10	**No one is perfect.** Is this an area of growth for you?

Remember, a score of zero (not applicable) in any area may lower your section score.

RELATIONAL CARE · SCORE

Stayed connected to friends and family members

Set aside time to spend with people I care about

Told people close to me that they were important

Apologized or made repairs when I was wrong

Expressed appreciation and thankfulness to others

Empathized with others or thought about problems from their perspective

Established limits and boundaries when necessary

TOTAL SCORE FOR THIS SECTION

SPIRITUAL CARE · SCORE

Attended religious or spiritual services

Spent time with others who share similar beliefs

Sought spiritual direction or guidance

Prayed or asked someone to pray for me

Practiced mindfulness and/or meditation

Identified important values and sought meaning in my life

Read or watched things that helped to inspire me

TOTAL SCORE FOR THIS SECTION

THE WEEK AHEAD

Daily self-care tracker

		M	T	W	T	F	S	S
PHYSICAL	Exercised for at least 10-15 minutes	✓						
	Took prescribed medications as directed	✗						
	Refrained from self-medicating							
	Got enough sleep							
	Ate balanced meals							
EMOTIONAL	Skillfully tolerated distressing moments							
	Validated my own thoughts, emotions, and experiences							
	Practiced self-compassion							
	Engaged in mindful breathing or breath counting							
	Observed and described feelings mindfully							
RELATIONAL	Practiced empathy and unconditional kindness							
	Let go of judgments about others							
	Used problem-solving skills to strengthen relationships							
	Said no and established limits when necessary							
	Expressed a mindful interest in others							
SPIRITUAL	Used prayer or meditation to help myself							
	Sought or created meaning in my life							
	Allowed myself to be inspired or to inspire others							
	Honored my values and beliefs							
	Attended religious or spiritual services							

MONDAY

DATE   /   /

Skills practiced

MINDFULNESS	EMOTION REGULATION	DISTRESS TOLERANCE	INTERPERSONAL EFFECTIVENESS

Things that I'm **thankful** for

1.
2.
3.

Goals I worked towards

Today's **shining moment**

Notes and reminders

DAYS SOBER OR NUMBER OF DAYS SINCE ENGAGING IN A HARMFUL OR DESTRUCTIVE BEHAVIOR

BEHAVIOR	DAYS SINCE

CONGRATULATIONS

You have completed **365 days**
of DBT Skills planning

PAST YEAR HIGHLIGHTS

Skills most practiced

MINDFULNESS	EMOTION REGULATION

Things that I'm **thankful** for

Goals I worked towards and/or achieved

1.

2.

3.

4.

5.

6.

7.

8.

9.

10.

DAYS SOBER

OR NUMBER OF DAYS SINCE ENGAGING IN A HARMFUL OR DESTRUCTIVE BEHAVIOR

BEHAVIOR	DAYS SINCE	BEHAVIOR	DAYS SINCE

DISTRESS TOLERANCE	INTERPERSONAL EFFECTIVENESS

Shining
moments/days

Notes and reminders

RECOMMENDED BOOKS AND WEBSITES

If you are feeling suicidal or are wanting to engage in self-destructive behaviors, please put this book down now and contact your doctor, therapist, or call your local emergency services.

Remember:
Asking for help is always skillful.

CRISIS/EMOTIONAL SUPPORT

7 Cups of Tea
7cupsoftea.com

Befrienders
befrienders.org

IMAlive
imalive.org

Lifeline Crisis Chat
crisischat.org/chat

National Suicide Prevention Lifeline
1-800-273-8255
suicidepreventionlifeline.org

RAINN
rainn.org

Samaritans
samaritans.org

Unsuicide
unsuicide.wikispaces.com

My local crisis line, peer support organization, or sponsor:

_____

_____

ORGANIZATIONS

Active Minds
activeminds.org

Clubhouse International
clubhouse-intl.org

Depression and Bipolar Support Alliance
dbsalliance.org

Mind
mind.org.uk

**National Alliance
on Mental Illness**
nami.org

**National Education Alliance for Borderline
Personality Disorder**
borderlinepersonalitydisorder.com

NEDA
nationaleatingdisorders.org

Recovery International
recoveryinternational.org

SMART Recovery
smartrecovery.org

DIALECTICAL BEHAVIOR THERAPY

Behavioral Tech
behavioraltech.org

Linehan Institute
linehaninstitute.org

My Dialectical Life
mydialecticallife.com

Now Matters Now
nowmattersnow.org

BOOKS

Aguirre, B. & Galen, G. (2015). *Coping with BPD: DBT and CBT Skills to Soothe the Symptoms of Borderline Personality Disorder.* Oakland, CA: New Harbinger Publications.

Aguirre, B. & Galen, G. (2013). *Mindfulness for borderline personality disorder: Relieve your suffering using the core skill of dialectical behavior therapy.* Oakland, CA: New Harbinger Publications.

Albers, S. (2009). *50 ways to soothe yourself without food.* Oakland, CA: New Harbinger Publications.

Blauner, S. R. (2003). *How I stayed alive when my brain was trying to kill me: One person's guide to suicide prevention.* New York, NY: HarperCollins.

Brach, T. (2004). *Radical acceptance: Embracing your life with the heart of a Buddha.* New York, NY: Bantam Books.

Frankl, V. E. (2006). *Man's Search for Meaning.* Boston, MA: Beacon Press.

Fruzzetti, A. E. (2004). *The high-conflict couple: A dialectical behavior therapy guide to finding peace, intimacy, and validation.* Oakland, CA: New Harbinger Publications.

Germer, C. K. (2009). *The mindful path to self-compassion: Freeing yourself from destructive thoughts and emotions.* New York, NY: Guilford Press.

Hall, K. D. (2014). *The emotionally sensitive person: Finding peace when your emotions overwhelm you.* Oakland, CA: New Harbinger Publications.

Kabat-Zinn, J. (2013). *Full catastrophe living: Using the wisdom of your body and mind to face stress, pain, and illness.* New York, NY: Bantam.

Kabat-Zinn, J. (1994). *Wherever you go, there you are: Mindfulness meditation for everyday life.* New York, NY: Hyperion.

Linehan, M. M. (2014). *DBT skills training handouts and worksheets* Second edition. New York, NY: The Guilford Press.

Linehan, M. M. (2014). *DBT skills training manual.* Second edition. New York, NY: The Guilford Press.

Neff, K. (2011). *Self-compassion: The proven power of being kind to yourself.* New York, NY: William Morrow.

Taitz, J. (2012). *End emotional eating: Using dialectical behavior therapy skills to cope with difficult emotions and develop a healthy relationship with food.* Oakland, CA: New Harbinger Publications.

Van Gelder, K. (2010). *The Buddha and the borderline: My recovery from borderline personality disorder through dialectical behavior therapy, Buddhism, and online dating.* Oakland, CA: New Harbinger Publications.

THE AUTHOR

Amanda L. Smith, LMSW, is founder of Hope for BPD where she provides treatment consultation and case management for clients located throughout the United States. Her career in mental health began when she served as the executive director of the Pinellas County, Florida affiliate of the National Alliance for Mental Illness (NAMI).

In 2007, she founded **Florida Borderline Personality Disorder Association**—a 501(c)(3) organization dedicated towards providing advocacy, education, and support for persons diagnosed with BPD and their families.

Amanda received her MSW at Baylor University and is currently working as a DBT therapist.

Her website is www.HopeForBPD.com

MORE FROM THE BPD WELLNESS SERIES

THE BPD WELLNESS SERIES

44.

45. **THE**

46. **BORDERLINE**

47. **PERSONALITY**

48. **DISORDER**

49. **WELLNESS**

50. **PLANNER**

51. **FOR FAMILIES**

52. **52** weeks of hope, inspiration, and mindful ideas for greater peace and happiness

Amanda L. Smith, LCSW

Available at **www.unhookedbooks.com**
and bookstores everywhere.